Shadforth a village histo

Shadforth Histo

Local Heritage *initiative*

Heritage Lottery Fund

Nationwide

The Countryside Agency

Local Heritage Initiative is a partnership between the Heritage Lottery Fund, Nationwide Buiding Society and the Countryside Agency

published © Shadforth History Group 2006

design Christina Unwin, Shadforth

printing Lintons Printers Ltd, Crook, County Durham

ISBN 0 9554164 0 X
978 0 9554164 0 8

contents

Introduction

This book has been written by Shadforth History Group, following a successful application by Shadforth Community Association to the Local Heritage Initiative for a grant to finance a history project.

The objectives of the project were to talk to residents of Shadforth, to record their memories of what life was like in the past in this small rural village on the outskirts of Durham City. We also wanted to produce a photographic archive and we appealed for old photographs. We have researched the local archives in the County Record Office to give some factual details to the history of the village. Our other objectives were to hold exhibitions, produce walk leaflets, erect an information board and set up a website at *www.lhi.org.uk*.

This book starts by giving an overall history of Shadforth and is then followed by a variety of different subjects, with contributions from residents as they remember them. The book is not intended to be a complete history of the village and, as much of it relies on people's memories, there may be some conflict or difference of opinions, as two people's views of events will never be the same. It will, hopefully, give a feel for the village and what life was like in the past and will keep alive people's memories.

Helen Grindley 2006

All photographs have been attributed to the owner for copyright reasons.

In general, the quotes in the book have not been attributed specifically to the speaker, as we are respecting some people's request to remain anonymous.

Copies of the interviews and our collection of photographs are available to view from Shadforth History Group.

Ordnance Survey maps of Shadforth

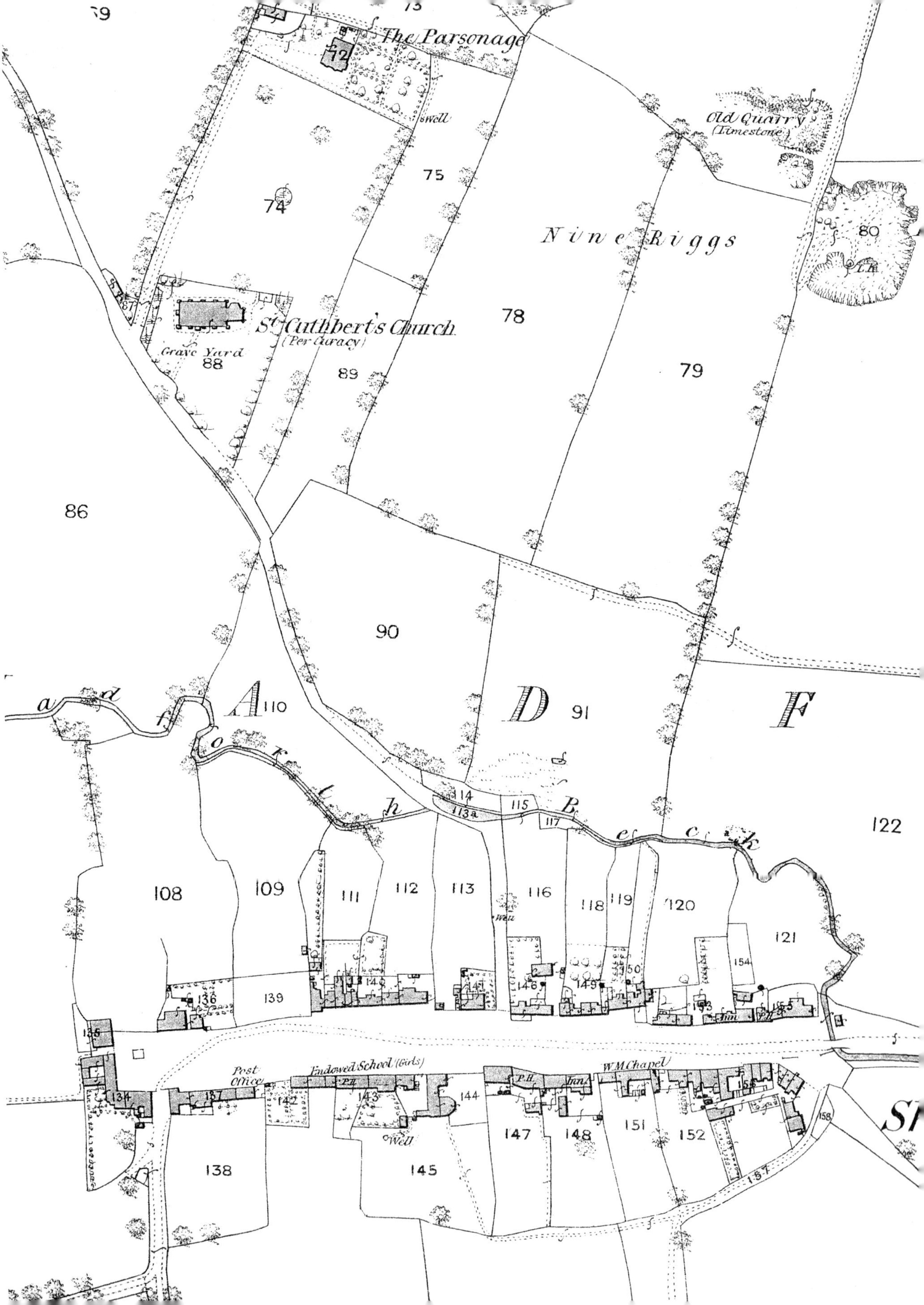
The Parsonage
72
Old Quarry
(Limestone)
Nine Riggs
St Cuthbert's Church
(Per Curacy)
Grave Yard
Well
A
D
F
Post Office
Endowed School (Girls)
W.M. Chapel
P.H.
Inn
74
75
78
79
80
86
87
88
89
90
91
108
109
110
111
112
113
113a
114
115
116
117
118
119
120
121
122
134
135
136
137
138
139
140
141
142
143
144
145
146
147
148
149
150
151
152
153
154
155
156
157
158

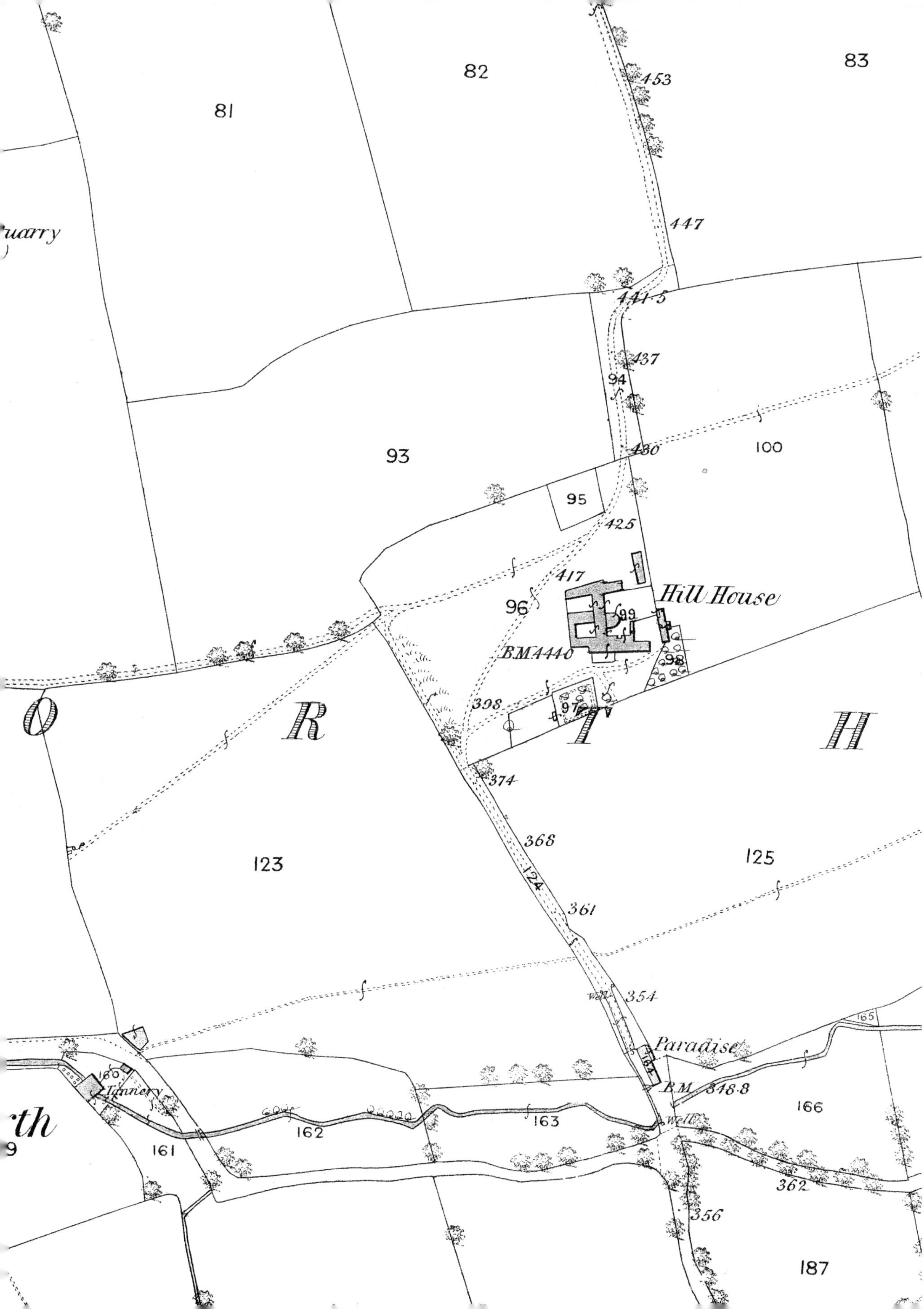
81
82
83
453
447
uarry
441·5
437
94
93
430
100
95
425
417
Hill House
96
99
B.M.444·0
98
398
97
O
R
T
H
374
368
123
125
124
361
354
Well
165
Paradise
164
160
Tinnery
B.M. 318·8
166
rth
9
162
163
Well
161
362
356
187

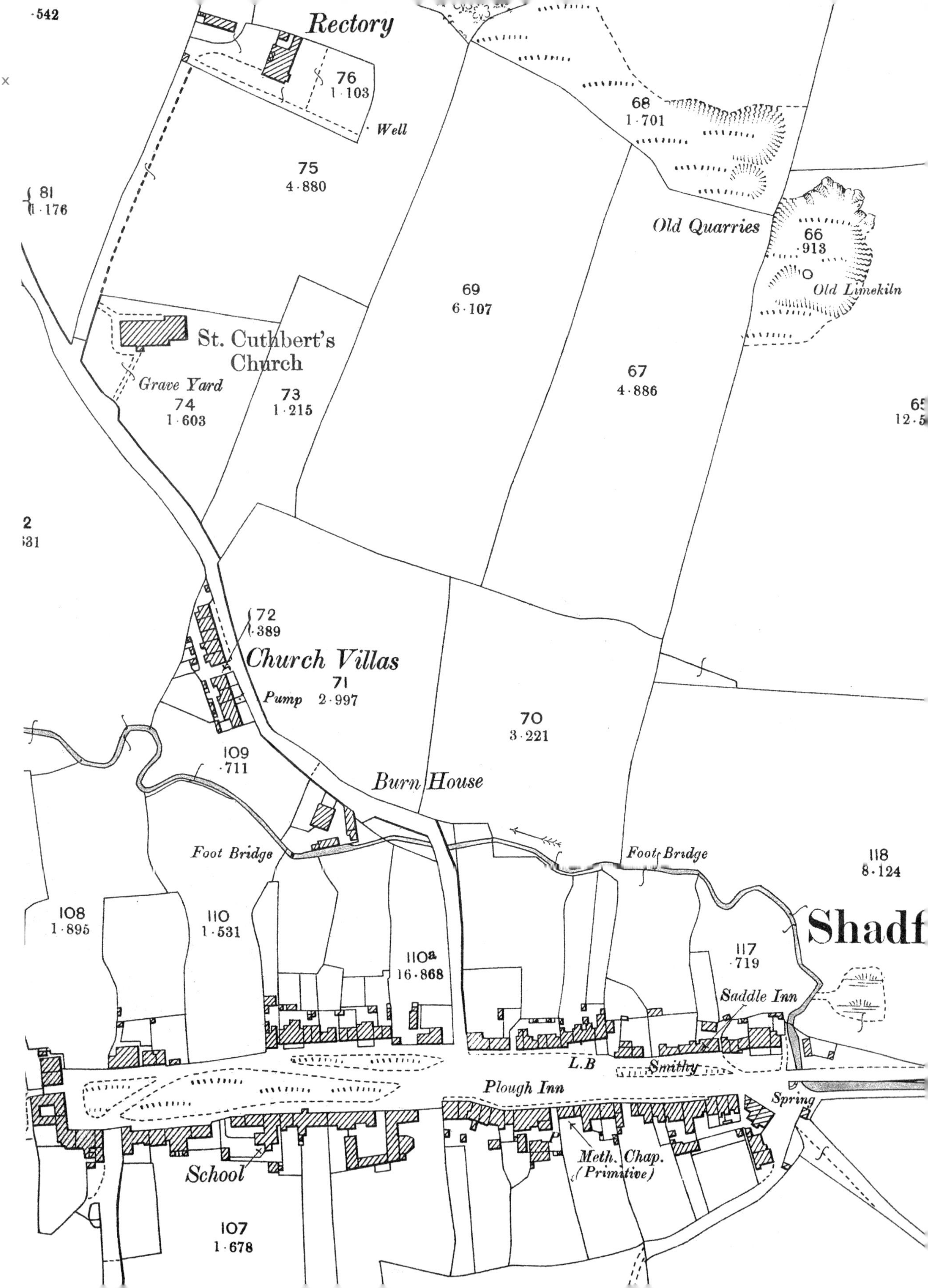

·542
Rectory
76
1·103
Well
68
1·701
75
4·880
81
1·176
Old Quarries
66
·913
Old Limekiln
69
6·107
St. Cuthbert's
Church
Grave Yard
74
1·603
73
1·215
67
4·886
65
12·5
2
·631
72
·389
Church Villas
71
Pump
2·997
70
3·221
109
·711
Burn House
Foot Bridge
Foot Bridge
118
8·124
108
1·895
110
1·531
110a
16·868
117
·719
Shadf
Saddle Inn
L.B
Smithy
Plough Inn
Spring
Meth. Chap.
(Primitive)
School
107
1·678

63
8·933
58
12·583
64
9·033
449
439
62
7·268
59
5·986
420
60
·951
Hill House
61
3·134
B.M.410·8
382
364
124
·444
125
10·608
119
11·841
F.P.
B.M.366·6
F.P.
Paradise
348
B.M.345·7
120
1·761
123
1·184
Ford
S h a d f
126
1·781
115
·471
359
355
127

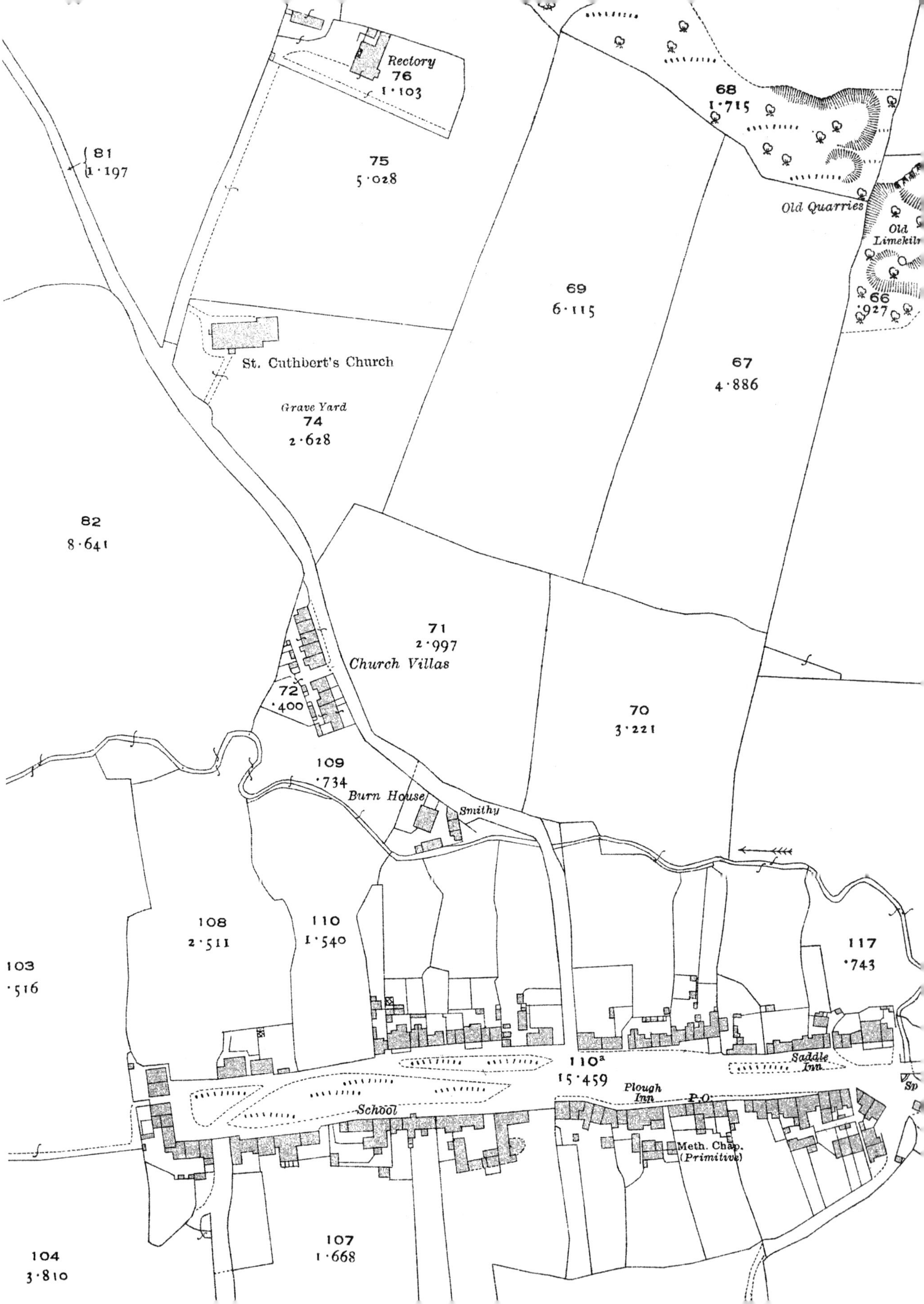

Rectory
76
1·103
68
1·715
81
1·197
75
5·028
Old Quarries
Old
Limekiln
66
·927
69
6·115
St. Cuthbert's Church
67
4·886
Grave Yard
74
2·628
82
8·641
71
2·997
Church Villas
72
·400
70
3·221
109
·734
Burn House
Smithy
108
2·511
110
1·540
117
·743
103
·516
110ª
15·459
Saddle
Inn
Plough
Inn
P.O.
School
Meth. Chap.
(Primitive)
107
1·668
104
3·810

63
8·933
449
64
9·033
439
62
7·268
59
5·896
420
61
1·615
60
2·570
Hill House
B.M. 410·8
Tanks
382
125
10·562
364
124
·434
119
13·602
F.P.
F.P.
B.M. 356·6
ndpump
348
Paradise
B.M. 345·7
Ford
forth
123
1·184
Shadforth Beck
116
2·540
115
·925
359
355

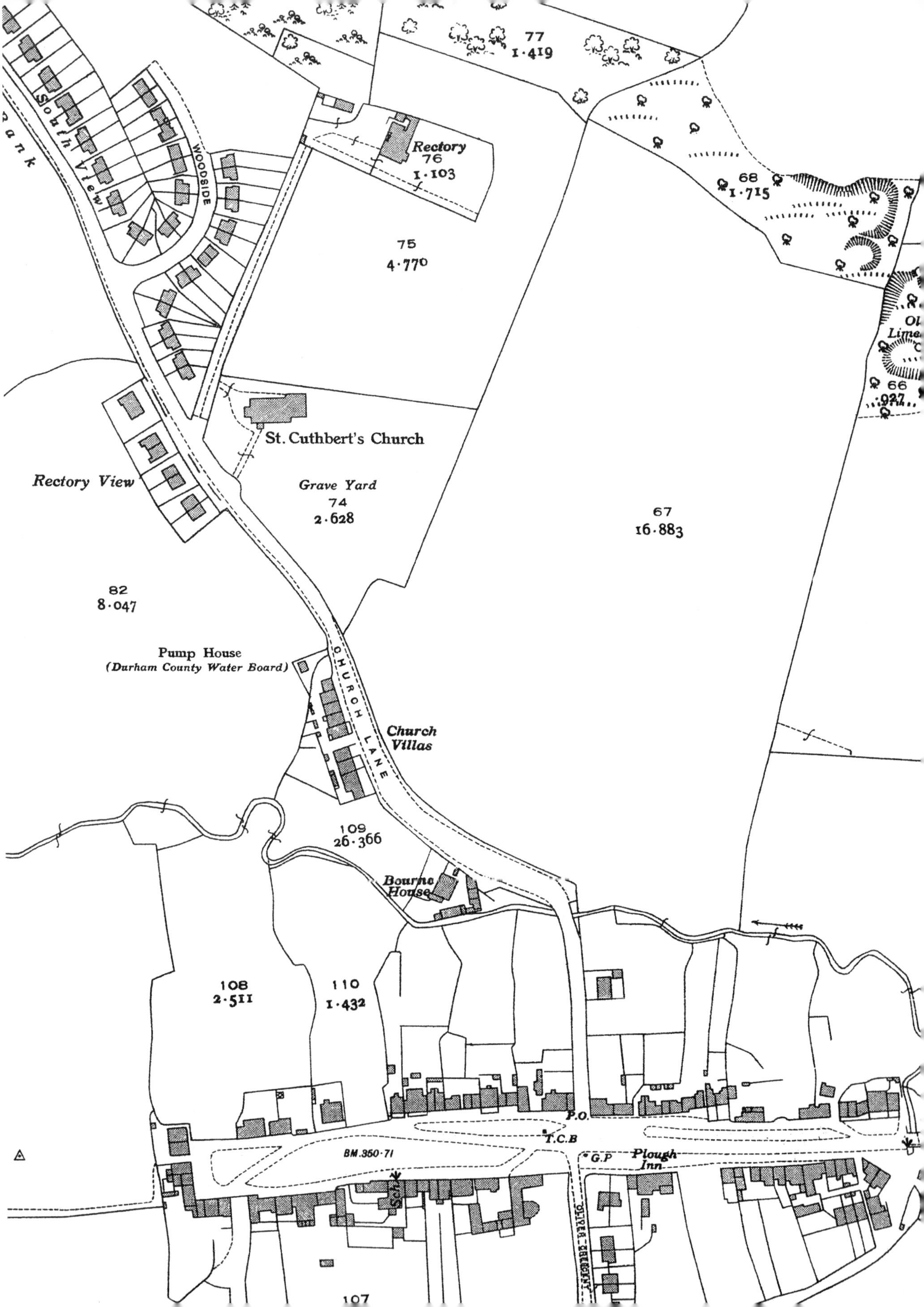
77
1·419
South View
WOODSIDE
Rectory
76
1·103
68
1·715
75
4·770
66
·927
St. Cuthbert's Church
Rectory View
Grave Yard
74
2·628
67
16·883
82
8·047
Pump House
(Durham County Water Board)
CHURCH LANE
Church Villas
109
26·366
Bourne House
108
2·511
110
1·432
P.O.
T.C.B
BM.350·71
G.P
Plough Inn
Sch
107

63
8·632
64
9·033
5
603
63a
·301
62
7·268
59
5·936
60 Tk.
2·530
BM.417·65
61
1·615
Tk.
Hill
House
Tank
Sheepwash
BM.373·66
F.P.
125
10·562
124 ·444
119
13·602
ndpump
F.P
Paradise
BM.341·89
126
1·788
Ford
F.B.
orth
115
·877
BM.335·22
123
1·184
S h a d f o r t h Beck
116
2·540

A history of Shadforth *William Chalder Wood*

This history article was originally written in 1991 and is reproduced here with some updating.

Shadforth parish lies four miles due east of Durham City and includes in its boundaries the village of Ludworth and part of Sherburn Hill.

The village of Shadforth itself nestles in the valley of Shadforth Beck and is a quiet settlement with mainly white and grey houses lining a long narrow green. The 19th-century church of St Cuthbert stands on rising ground on the opposite side of the beck, near the relatively modern additions to the village of the council houses and a few private houses in front of the church.

A mile upstream from the village is the great gaunt ruin of Ludworth Tower, which guards the approach to the tiny 19th-century mining village of Ludworth. The mine closed several years ago and all that remains of the site is a grassed area and a pine-covered landscaped hillock.

The Tower formed part of a larger manor house which was fortified by Roger Holden in 1422, licence to crenellate being given by Bishop Langley, probably as a reward, since Holden was a man of some importance in the Bishop's service. Around the manor house was a medieval village, mentioned in 1209, but by the late 1400s it had vanished, possibly cleared away to make the land available for sheep.

Whatever the reason, no one knows exactly where the site of the village was, but Tower Farm has stood in the area ever since the manor house fell into ruin. All that remains are the west wall, a vaulted basement, three windows, traces of fireplaces and a winding stone staircase.

To the north of Shadforth, some 300 feet above the village and one mile away, stands the village of Sherburn Hill. Like the present day Ludworth, it is essentially a 19th-century foundation created to house miners after the sinking of a pit in the 1830s. It was once a bustling community; now, the mine having closed, it is a shadow of its former self, many of the old pit terraced

Shadforth in the 1920s, looking west, across the village green to 'Top End'. Brown's Buildings, at the far end of the village, have since been demolished. The gable building on the left is the school
Johnston postcard [Bill Errington]

cottages having been demolished. It is served by four shops, including a post office*, a public house, a Working Men's Club and, spiritually, by a Methodist Chapel and a thriving Salvation Army Church.

There is evidence from aerial photography that the first inhabitants of the parish area were Iron Age farmers. Small settlements of Celtic families, possibly dating from about 100 BC, have been spotted; one about a quarter of a mile southwest of Ludworth, one about half a mile north-northwest of Shadforth in the region of Crime Rigg and a third on top of the high spur near Running Waters quarry. Until archaeological digs can be made, however, nothing is certain about the sites.

It is known that, just as Ludworth had a 'lost' medieval village, there was an earlier Anglo-Saxon settlement of Shadforth. There is documentary evidence that the village existed before the Norman Conquest, perhaps as far back as AD 800. The name 'Shadforth' derives from the Old English word *sceald*, meaning shallow. The derivation is proved by the spellings used in the Boldon Book of 1183; the name appears as *Shaldeford* and *Shaldeforth*, or 'shallow ford'. It is not known why the early Anglo-Saxon settlement disappeared, but one possibility is that it suffered as a result of the devastation of the 11th-century harrying of County Durham by the Scots, Vikings and Norman armies, followed by disease and starvation. The village in its present form may well have been created on the site of the devastated settlement, which could explain why no trace of the old village has been found, so it appears that the 'new' Shadforth dates from about 1080.

About a hundred years later, in 1183, the Boldon Book was written. This was a survey created for Hugh de Puiset, Bishop of Durham, and showed returns of all his holdings, lands, rents and customs in the Bishopric. It tells us that Shadforth, together with Quarrington, Cassop, North Sherburn and South Sherburn (the present Sherburn House) formed the district of Quarringtonshire. The shires of the Boldon Book are believed to show the antiquity of our Old English territorial system, being small estates of townships and other holdings dependent on a chief settlement – Quarrington in our case – where the Bishop's own farm was situated. It was to this farm that the villeins of the shire, bond tenant farmers, did their compulsory labour services, paid their rents and dues, and made court appearances when required.

Shadforth would seem to have had about fifteen villeins and one free tenant, Thomas of Shadforth, each holding two oxgangs of land (60 Durham acres), the equivalent of about 96 modern acres. Each tenant was required to pay 2s 6d taxation (16d carriage money and half a scot-chalder of oats) five wagonloads of wood, two hens and ten eggs. He also had to work for the Bishop three days a week for the whole year, except for Easter and Whitsun weeks and thirteen days at Christmas. If necessary, each year, the villeins had to build one house forty feet long and fifteen feet wide and, if they did this, they were exempt from 4d carriage money. Thomas, the freeman, as a highly ranked tenant, went 'on missions for the Bishop', carrying messages and legal documents. Assuming an average of one wife and two children per tenant, it would seem that the village population was around sixty-four souls.

*The post office has since closed.

Little else is known of Shadforth until Bishop Hatfield's survey (1345–1381), when we are told that the land held in Shadforth by Sir Raph Eure formerly belonged to Thomas de Teesdale and that there were now two free tenants, Isabell Boner and Thomas, the heir to John Freeman. The bond tenants were Robert Alleynson, John Bedyk, John Greveson, John Ludworth, Thomas Jonson, Thomas Perrison, William Smyth, William Robinson, Thomas of Sherburn, Thomas Huetson, William Wardon and William Alleynson.

Each bond tenant paid 23s 4d every year, as well as six bushels of oats, two hens and ten eggs, to the Bishop. Between them, they also paid 6s for a milk cow, 25s 6d for cornage (the right to pasture) 12s for wagonloads of wood, 2s for the common furnace, 2s 8d for the ale-toll and 6s 8d towards the pinder, the keeper of the village pound. All this in return for the tenancy of two oxgangs of land. Robert Taillour and Margaret de Hall held the cottages formerly belonging to the common forge.

Some two hundred years later, in 1587, tenants of Shadforth included Roger Lakenby, Christopher Pearson, George Taylor, Nicholas Hall, Richard Huntley, Alice Wilkinson, Ralph Hall, Robert Meaborne, Jerrard Swalwell and Henry Wright. The Lackenby family also held considerable leaseholds, while the freehold belonging to William Hall, a yeoman, descended to William Swalwell.

About this time, the farmers were wanting to reorganise their land holdings into more easily worked areas. Up to now, each tenant had tilled his lands in the medieval way, that is, in strips of lands scattered over the three huge open cornfields of the village. A great deal of time was wasted with much travelling to and fro between strips. Pressure for land re-organisation grew throughout the country and Acts of Enclosure were passed, enabling the tenants of Shadforth to re-arrange their strips into consolidated blocks. No doubt there was much wheeling and dealing among themselves to try to get the best bargain in the way of good land.

Having finally agreed upon their new plots, the farmers enclosed their fields from 1635 onwards. The enclosures gave the countryside around the village its present-day shape, with its irregular fields and hedges though, sadly, in the name of progress, many of the hedges have been ripped out again over the last forty years.

The yeoman farmers and tenants involved in the share-out of land were William Swallwell, William Huntley, Philip Haddock (an ancestor of the writer), Richard Edrington, William Taylor, William Swallwell Junior, William Edrington (the Greve of Shadforth), William Hall, Ralph Huntley, Robert Meaburne, Robert Swalwell, Thomas Huntley, Jane Dent, Simon Lackenby and James Swallwell.

It was around this time that houses in the village were being built increasingly of the local stone rather than of wood. A few of these buildings still stand, although most of the present houses are later than the 1600s. The outlying farmhouses, such as Oxclose, Fat Close, Crime Rigg and Strawberry, dated from just after the enclosures, even though by now they have been added to or rebuilt.

The next glimpse of who lived in Shadforth comes just seven years later, in 1642. That was the year when all the male population over the age of eighteen years were required to sign an affirmation that they were of the Protestant religion. Those who did not sign were called 'recusants', and were mainly Roman Catholics. Although the names of the following Shadforth men varied in spelling, as was usual in those days, it is obvious that the named people of the enclosures are still the same men of the Protestation: Symon Leakenbie, William Hall, Richard Hedringtoune, Robert Meaburne, William Smith, Raph Hall, Christopher Chetter, Thomas Ree, Richard Cotsworth, William Hedringtoune, William Swalwell, Phillip Haddocke, William Huntlie, George Dobbinson, William Swalwell and Ambrose Gambsbie. Servants, probably farm workers, Nicholas Smith, George Smith, John Taylour, Robert Burd, Raph Bunteene, James Rannison, William Nattbie, John Hall, William Hall and George White also signed.

From the hamlet of Ludworth, William, James, John, Marmaduk and George Swalwell and Robert Darntoune signed, as did their servants Raph Burd, Raph Burd (the younger), Thomas Sheretoune and Richard Elge. Raph and Thomas Huntlie, although both attending Pittington Church, which was the parish church for Shadforth, did not sign.

Life in the village must have continued in much the same way for the next two hundred years, but changes inevitably came. In 1801, the population was about 180 and gradually rose to 336 in 1841. In 1828, there were fourteen farmers in Shadforth and Ludworth, some of whom were named: Israel Alderson of Cassop Smithy Farm, William Branson at Deanhouse, John Clark at Ludworth and Running Waters, Joseph Johnson at Fatclose House, Thomas Swinns at Strawberry Hill and Thomas Darling at Hill House. John Huntley kept the Board Inn, while Matthew Gardner had the Wheatsheaf, Thomas Moore was the schoolmaster, William Jameson and Richard Wearmouth were blacksmiths and John Brown was the cartwright and joiner.

One outstanding event for the village was the consecration of the new church of St Cuthbert in Shadforth by Bishop Maltby on 5th August 1839. The first vicar, Reverend R G L Blenkinsopp, and churchwardens Henry Newby and John Huntley, signed a tablet over the doorway inside the church, which gave details of the erection.

The most momentous occasion, however, followed in 1841. A Court held in Council at Buckingham Palace, Her Majesty Queen Victoria being present, on 8th May, ordered that the ancient parish of Pittington, which included the constabularies of (1) Pittington, Elemore and Hetton on the Hill (2) Shadforth and Ludworth (3) Sherburn, should be divided into two separate parishes for ecclesiastical purposes; one part to be Pittington and the northwest part of Sherburn to remain attached to the original church at Hallgarth, Pittington; the other part to consist of the whole of Shadforth township, including Ludworth and the rest of Sherburn township, to be served by the new church in Shadforth.

At a stroke, the population of Shadforth rose from 336 before 8th May 1841 to over two thousand people. The 1851 census showed that 2,856 people inhabited 540 houses in the new parish. This tremendous increase was due partly to the extended area but mainly to the new pit villages built in Sherburn, Sherburn Hill and Ludworth, where miners and their families flooded in. Although this changed the character of the parish as a whole, Shadforth itself, enclosed by steep hills and out of sight of the collieries, kept its rural aspect.

The 1854 edition of Fordyce described Shadforth as having houses built on each side of the main road and green in irregular fashion, many having floors of rough stone slabs or gravelly concrete, often found in the older cottages of County Durham. There were three public houses, a skinnery, a blacksmith's forge, cartwright's and joiner's shops, as well as a Methodist (formerly Presbyterian) Chapel, on the site of which the present Village Hall stands, and a Dame School.

By 1860, we know that John Thursby was the postmaster of Shadforth and Richard Earle was the fell-monger with the skinnery. New inns had appeared, albeit in old houses; as well as The Wheatsheaf (landlord Thomas Ritson) there wasThe Black Horse (John Carter) The Plough (Robert Jordison) The Red Lion (Nicholas Jenkins) and The Saddle (Edward Baldwin). John Clark farmed Oxclose; William Clark Fatclose; John Proud Strawberry Hill; Joseph Robinson High Croft House; Matthew Robson High House; John Sanderson Shadforth Farm; and Catherine Shotton Crime Rigg. The majority of Shadforth folk still followed the ways of the farming community, but several miners' families lived there too. They would have worked at any of the surrounding collieries – Cassop, Sherburn Hill or Ludworth.

The National School, built 1863–4, with Mr Matthew Barron as headmaster, superseded the Dame School. Mr Thomas Brown was a long-standing headteacher of note in the 1920s, 30s and 40s. The last headteacher, Mrs Reveler, had the sad task of supervising the closure of the school in 1964, owing to the lack of children in the village, at a time when Durham Education Authority was reorganising schools on the basis of numbers.

A Reading Room and Lending Library were established in 1887, possibly at the instigation of the Misses Carr-Standish, who were the Ladies of the Manor and the chief landowners alongside John Clark, Richard Nicholson, Thomas Hooper, Miss Blenkinsopp and Mr D Botherell in the 1890s.

Shadforth was still a thriving village. Jeffrey Young was postmaster, and the Whittingham brothers had become established stonemasons. The Plough and The Saddle inns did good trade; Thomas Hutchinson was landlord of The Saddle.

At the turn of the century, Thomas Hutchinson was in great demand as the local 'pig-sticker', setting out with his lethal implements and dressed in his top hat. Other local characters included old Mr Thubron, coffin-maker and cartwright, who had a fearsome black beard and always wore a shawl around his shoulders. Harry Oliver, another slaughterer and butcher, of Low Croft Farm, well known for hard drinking, fell off his cart on the way home one day and killed himself. One pastime, now happily forgotten, was sparrow shooting, which was carried out by netting haystacks when the birds were roosting in them at night. Next morning, when the nets were loosened, the birds were blasted with shotguns.

There were wind-pumps around the valley to provide water for some of the farms on higher ground and a well at the east end of the village, with steps down to the water-level, for the rest of the inhabitants before piped water was laid on.

There was a corn-mill, believed to date from the 17th century, standing half a mile northwest of Shadforth, near the now deserted farmstead of Cold Knuckles. The mill was of interest, partly because of its age and remote situation but mainly because of the way it was worked. Although it stood on a small grassy bank near the beckside, it was not, as you might expect, operated by the beck's flow, but by a deep sluice cut into the top of the bank. This sluice, now partly filled in as the years have gone by, can still be traced some 275 metres (300 yards) back to a boggy area, where it collected water from field ditches and dykes which, in turn, were partly fed by a large pond near Long Myers Farm. The mill's position meant that it could be approached only by three circuitous routes: from the village along Running Waters Lane, turning right past Cold Knuckles; from the east end of Sherburn Village via the moor; and from Crime Rigg farm across the fields. It was last lived in by members of the Crawford family, grandchildren of the noted coal-owner Thomas Crawford of Littletown House, in 1925. It was demolished in 1930.

Two reminders of ancient days are to be found in the names of Witch Hill and Signing Bank, both near the south boundary of the parish. Although there is no documentation, legend has it that Witch Hill was the site for burnings and hangings hundreds of years ago. Signing Bank, running from Witch Hill westwards on the A181 road to Durham, was the point on the road where pilgrims, travelling from the coast to visit the shrine of St Cuthbert, first caught sight of Durham Cathedral and made the sign of the cross.

The two World Wars took their drastic toll of the young men of the parish, but life had to go on. There were, however, changes taking place in agricultural methods, between the Wars and more especially after the Second World War, which were to have a great effect on the character of the community. Farms, which had each employed several men, boys and girls, became highly mechanised. The resultant loss of jobs caused a number of

North Side
[Bill Errington]

above **Looking towards the west end of the village, in around 1926**
Johnston postcard [Bill Errington]

left **By the 1930s, telegraph poles have appeared**
Johnston postcard [Bill Errington]

below **A view from the east end of the village, known as 'Bottom End', in the 1930s. The Saddle Inn is on the right**
Johnston postcard [Stan Foord]

From Rectory View, looking down to Church Villas, in the 1930s or 1940s
Johnston postcard
[George Nairn]

villagers to drift away to find other work; associated trades, the smithy, the skinnery, and the cartwrights', joiners' and the builders' workshops, closed; the village appeared to be stagnating. Only one general dealer cum Post Office remained but it, too, had closed from lack of trade by 1978. The Plough Inn alone survives.

Of all the people previously dependent upon the farms and country trades, only the farmers and their families follow the traditional life. While the number of farms has stayed very much the same over the centuries, the names of the farmers have changed. The ten farms of the parish are held as follows: Dene House, S W Foord; Crime Rigg, E Gilchrist; High House, C Maddison; Hill House, G Johnston; Tower Farm, C Simpson; Paradise Farm, J Shepherd; Oxclose, J Brass; Fatclose, Eley Brothers; High Croft, G H Gilson; and Smithy Farm, J Johnson.* J Gatenby has a small-holding with sheep and horses, but owns a good deal of the land around the village.

Most of the rest of the working residents have jobs outside Shadforth, mainly in the Durham City area, presenting a stark contrast to the self-contained and tightly-knit community of yesteryear.

Rectory View was built in the 1920s and in the 1930s the Council built a small estate of houses north of the church called South Avenue and Woodside. Over the last thirty years, a few new houses have been built around the green, but only where there had been buildings before, because Shadforth has been declared a Conservation Area. There has also been some in-filling down Chare Lane and on the site of the former piggery at Bourne House. Several newcomers have trickled into the village with their young families, bringing new blood and ideas into the community.

The village is very attractive and has had trees planted on the green and on the outskirts. It is peaceful, quiet and pleasant and, if developers can be kept at bay, it should so remain as a gem of our heritage for future generations.

* Some farm owners have since changed.

South Avenue, built by the Council in 1935
[Margaret Iveson]

Joyce and her mother, Vera Parker, at 20 Woodside in 1948. The Grey Houses, or Airey Houses, are in the background
[Joyce St Julien]

left to right **Joyce and Eileen Parker with grandad, Joe Smith, around 1950**
[Joyce St Julien]

Joe Smith with his dogs, Nell and Lady, at 20 Woodside in the late 1940s
[Joyce St Julien]

Joyce Parker feeding pigeons at 20 Woodside in the late 1940s
[Joyce St Julien]

Rebuilding Shadforth in 1958
left to right **Michael and Louise McEnaeny, Polly Errington, Freddie McEnaeny, Billy Errington and Bobby Summers**
[Louise McEnaeny]

Medieval fields and enclosures

William Chalder Wood

The medieval fields of Shadforth

Shadforth was a farming village from ancient times. The Old English settlers came here, around AD 600, to a heavily-wooded countryside. Within fifty or so years, they had cleared the land around the village to cultivate many strips of land in large open fields.

They used four oxen to pull each heavy plough. Every peasant farmer had several strips in every open field, each strip being 220 yards long and 11 yards wide (a furlong meaning a 'furrow long'), amounting to about 80 acres.

They also had the use of common land on 'The Hills', 'North Hills' and in 'The Dene', consisting of moor, scrubland, meadows for grazing and woodland for timber and firewood. These lay outside the open fields. 'Ox Pasture' was an enclosed field that was kept clear of animals until the hay had been gathered in, and then only oxen were allowed to graze there.

After a thousand years of using this ancient agricultural method, the farmers wanted to reorganise their holdings to make their work easier. A Parliamentary Act of Enclosure made this possible.

The medieval fields of Shadforth before 1635

[after Bill Wood]

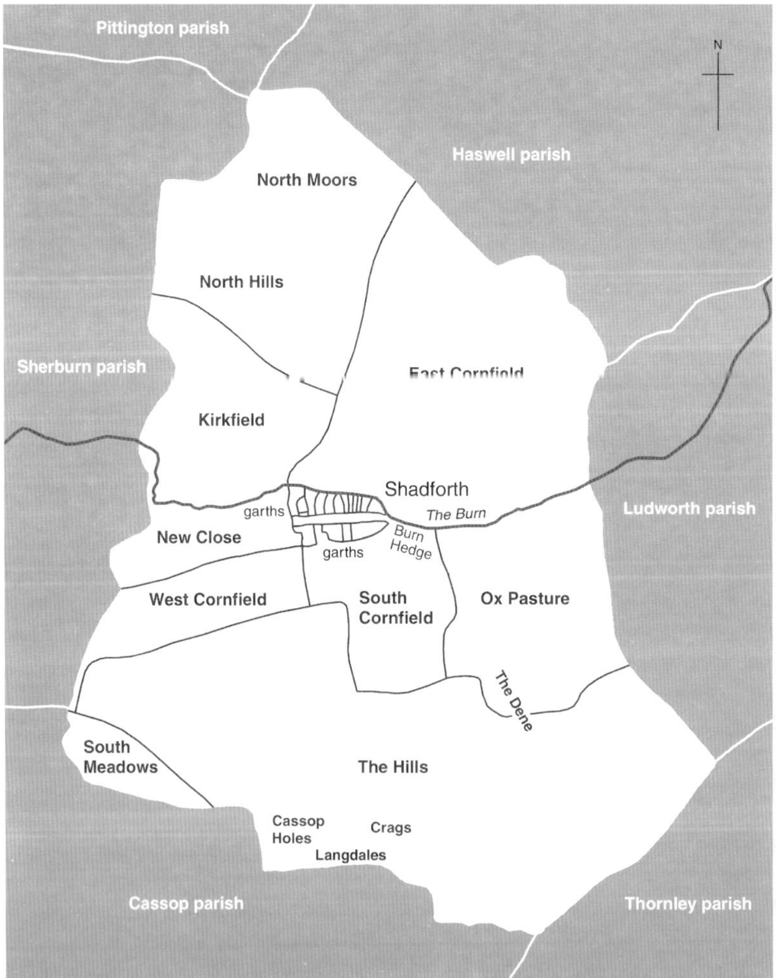

Shadforth enclosures 1635

In 1635, the Shadforth farmers were able to enclose their allotted portions of land from the five open fields known as 'Kirk Field' (held for the priest of Pittington Church), 'East Cornfield', 'West Cornfield', 'South Cornfield' and 'New Close'. The map below shows the new divisions of land and the names of people in the village who farmed them at that time. The old open fields have gone.

The farmers enclosed their allotments of land with hawthorn hedges, making many small fields in the process, some of which survive to this day, giving the countryside around the village its present appearance. They soon built substantial farmhouses on their new land, the sites of which are shown on the map.

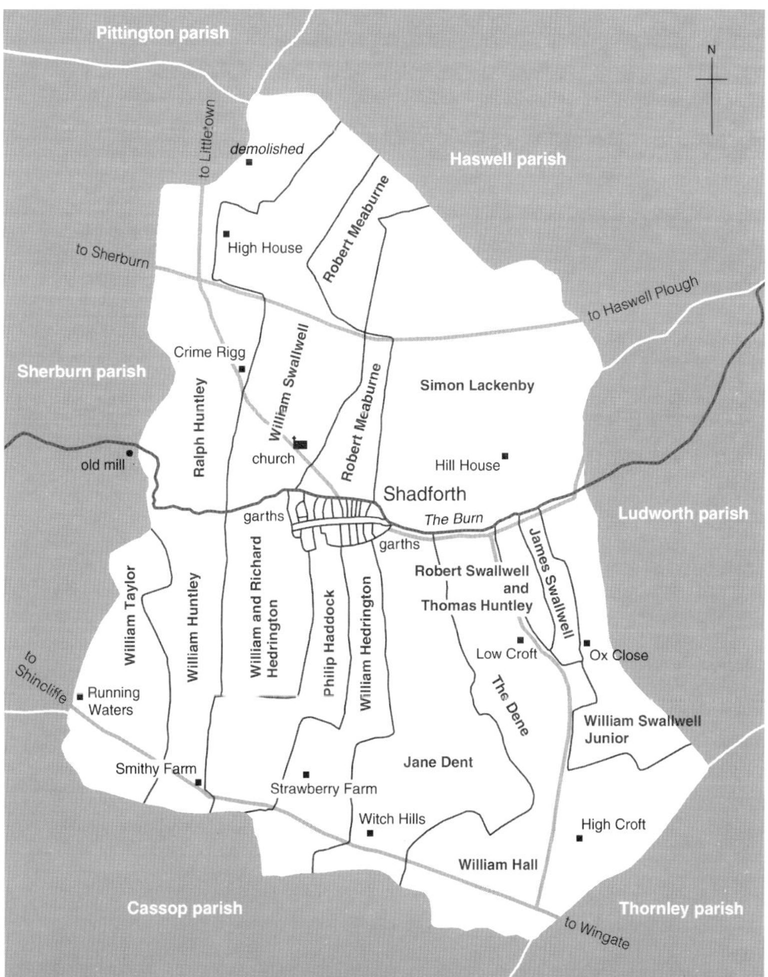

The Shadforth Enclosure Awards of 1635
[after Bill Wood]

▪ site of old farmhouse, built after 1635

present road

0 1/4 1/2 mile

Shadforth Enclosure Awards 1635

Between Will Swallwell, Wm Huntley, Phillip Haddock, Richd Edrington, Wm Taylor, Wm Swallwell Jnr (Ludworth), Wm Edrington Greve of Shadforth, Wm Hall, Ralph Huntley, Robt Meaburne, Robt Swallwell, Thomas Huntley, Jaine Dent, versus Simon Lackenby, Wm Hall Jun. and James Swallwell.

Awards

Wm Swallwell Jnr of Ludworth – Ox pasture 58 ac. 1 Rood 27 poles
Bounded on E. with Ludworth Boundary, on S. with Wm Hall's Grounds. W. by James Swallwell and N. Simon Lackenby.

James Swallwell 20-0-16
Bounded on E. by Wm Swallwell Jun, S. William Hall, W. Robt Swallwell, N. Simon Lackenby.

Robt Swallwell and Thos Huntley 11-3-13
Bounded E. James Swallwell, S. Wm Hall, W. Wm Hall, N. S Lackenby.

William Hall 221-0-0
Bounded by E. Robt Swallwell, James Swallwell + Ludworth + Thornley, W. Cassop and N. J Dents and S Lackenby.

Jane Dent 148-1-36
East part of South Cornfield and part Oxpasture (W. side of the Dene), part of Hill called Langdales with Craggs. Bounded E. Wm Hall, S. Cassop, W. Wm Hedrington, N. Burne Hedge and town Garths.

Wm Hedrington 79-1-10
E. half of West part of South Cornfield + part of hills i.e. Cassop Holes. Bounded E. with J Dent, S. Cassop, W. Phillip Haddock, N. garthes of S. side of Town.

Phillip Haddock 71+3+24
W. part of South Cornfield and part of Hills.
Bounded E. Wm. Edrington, S. Cassop, W. Wm Huntley, N. Wm and Richd Edrington.

Wm and Rich Hedrington 68+0+0
E. part of New Close, E. part of W. Cornfield and part of hills.
Bounded E. with West End of Town, S. Wm Taylors garth and Ph. Haddocks Ground, W. with Phill Haddock's ground with Wm. Huntley, N. Wm Swallwell.

Wm Huntley 71+0+0
Middle part New Close, Mid part of West Cornfield, part of hills and S. Meadows. Bounded by E. with W. Edrington and Ph. Haddock, S. with Cassop, W. Wm Taylors N. Ralph Huntley.

Wm Taylor 73+0+26
W. part of New Close and W. part of W. Cornfield, W. part of hills and S. Meadows. Bounded E. Wm Huntley, S. Cassop, W. and N. Sherburn.

Ralph Huntley 140+3+36
W. part of Kirk Field, W. part of N. hills, W. part of Moor.

Wm Swallwell 142+1+20
E. part of Kirkfields and part of moors.

Robt. Meaburne 71+2+34
[No description, but it is north of the burn (beck) above the Northside Town garths and bounded by William Swallwell's and Simon Lackenby's land]

Simon Lackenby 220+3+16
N. part of East Cornfield.

Field area names

Ludworth – Thornley – Cassop–Sherburn boundaries

North Moors – North Hills – Kirkfield – East Cornfield – The Burn – Burne Hedge – Town Garths – New Close – West Cornfield – South Cornfield – Ox Pasture – The Dene – South Meadows – Langdales Hill with Craggs – Cassop Holes

Hearth taxes of 1674 *William Chalder Wood*

Four hundred years ago, everyone in the country was taxed on the number of hearths they had in his dwelling place. Only those who were poverty-stricken were excused. The following names are those on the Shadforth roll.

taxpayer *solvent*	**hearths**
Widow Swalwell	1
Widow Lackenby	3
Wm Errington	1
James Watson	2
Rob Whitfeild	2
Rob Wilson	2
Wm Taylor	1
Widow Huntley	1
Jo Watson	1
Wm Errington	2
Rich Errington	2
Rob Errington	1
Bart Ingraham	1
Thos Carton	1
Widow Swalwell	2
Ellinor Swalwell	2
James Lister	1
Geo Simpson	2
Peter Clerke	1
Jo Clerke	1
Hen Dobson	1

non-payer *non-solvent*	**hearths**
ffran Huntly	1
Widow Huntly	1
Widow Gamsbye	1
Jo Bullocke	1
Wm Markham	1
Wm Wilson	1
Wm Hudson	1
Hugh Bowman	1
Jo Morras	1
Wm Man	1

Shadforth township ancient boundary survey 1993

William Chalder Wood

In 1993, Durham County Environmental Department asked for help in making a survey of all the ancient township and parish boundaries in the county. Its purpose was to find out what condition the old hedges, which originally formed the boundaries, were in. In the case of Shadforth, the boundary would have been created by the Old English settlers some time between AD 600 and 800.

As a Durham Countryside Voluntary Ranger, I offered to make a survey of Shadforth township. In the event, I completed that and, because of poor response to the task by others, went on to do the same for Ludworth, Sherburn, and Sherburn House townships. My assignment was to pinpoint the line of the boundary, using old maps, and to record everything I could discover about its physical signs.

That meant walking the actual border line and tracing all evidence of mounds, ditches, lynchets (ridges formed by ancient ploughing on slopes), marker stones, landmark trees, remaining hedges and anything else of interest. This included all species of shrubs, trees and flowers seen in the hedges and embankment. I had to record everything I discovered, and the information was to be transferred onto a large map, using various symbols and code numbers. It took me three weeks to map and record the seven and a half mile boundary of Shadforth.

I found out that there is an earth embankment almost all the way around the township boundary. It varies in height from about 0.5 to 2 metres (1 foot 6 inches to six feet). Where there is no embankment, natural ditches and becks form the line. Most of the remaining hedges showed signs of ancient layering, but there are several stretches where the hedge has completely vanished and fences have been erected.

I began my survey near the junction of the minor road leading uphill from Paradise Cottages and the A181 Shincliffe road. My first find was a small pit-fall fault on the Cassop side of the boundary. Other notable features I came across included eight large stones placed around the township perimeter, usually about 40 x 30 x 30 centimetres (about 16 x 12 x 12 inches) in size; the two largest were about 70 x 40 x 30 centimetres (28 x 16 x 12 inches). Many smaller field stones, cleared by farmers, lined other parts of the boundary.

Trees and shrubs on the borderline included hawthorn, ash, alder, blackthorn, sycamore, elm, willow, sallow, elder, hazel, guelder rose, holly, honeysuckle, woody nightshade, bramble, dog-rose (briar), ivy and whin (gorse). There is a notable line of ash trees making part of the Cassop–Shadforth boundary; it is shown on the Ordnance Survey map as 'ash'.

Finally, the most outstanding tree to be found is by the beck, near Running Waters, next to a natural spring. It is four and a half metres (15 feet) in circumference; an ancient willow that has been pollarded over the years.

It was a fascinating experience to discover this timeworn boundary, which I felt almost brought me in touch with the township's original settlers from so long ago.

The village hall and Shadforth Community Association

The village hall, situated on South Side, is in a central position of the village, next to the Plough Inn (recently renamed 'The Shadforth Plough'). It was built on the site of the old Methodist Chapel. Villagers are still very proud of their village hall, as it was built over a number of years in the early 1950s, using voluntary labour from the villagers themselves and, as such, it belongs to the villagers even today.

The 'Grand Opening' of the village hall was reported in the *Durham County Advertiser* on Friday 20th September 1957, under the title 'The Fruits of Their Labours' and 'Shadforth's Great Day'. In the report, it stated that the idea of a village hall went back as far as 1950. Villagers realised they needed a place to hold meetings, dances and whist drives. Shadforth Community Association was formed, and their first decision was that they would build the hall themselves.

The Grand Opening of the village hall

'A wonderful example of what voluntary work can achieve can be seen at Shadforth, where villagers have built their own Welfare Hall. Pictures were taken when Mr Ralph M Allison, Castle Eden, officially opened the building. While below are men of Shadforth who can feel proud of their efforts.'
Durham County Advertiser 20th September 1957
[Stuart Watt]

It was estimated that £1600 was needed to build the hall and, although some grants were given, the majority of the money was raised by voluntary donations and money-raising events. The local Women's Institute, described as one of the village's most energetic bodies, ran a series of money-making efforts which put £133 into the fund.

Other fund-raising events included social evenings and dances, as Sheila Wilson (née Davis), a young girl at the time, recalls:

We started to have social evenings in the school and they were a huge success; so much so, the school became too small for the numbers coming in and they decided to hold these weekly dances in Sherburn Hill Community Centre – it was called the Welfare Hall. These dances took off. My father was the MC. I remember these dances used to be packed out and they used to run buses to take people back to the Sherburn Road Estate, because a lot of young people came from there. We used to have refreshments at these 'do's – my mother was always making scones – and charge for them as well. We had live bands. If anyone wanted to do a turn, you were allowed to. I can remember my dad playing the piano and I used to sing. So that is how they made most of their money.

There seems to have been a wealth of local talent to provide entertainment, as other residents recall:

There were dances in the village school on Saturday nights to raise money for the village hall and my husband, Wylam, used to play the drums at these dances.

My husband, Albert, used to play the drums, with Dickie Stoker on the piano, to raise money for the village hall.

When sufficient money was available, work started and, as the *Advertiser* reported, 'The village tradesmen then came into their own and, helped by a labour force of unskilled but keen workers, the building began.'

One resident remembers:

My husband was a boot and shoe repairer, so he did not do shifts like the miners. He helped as a labourer, digging the drains. He was there every night. I can remember a photo of him and the other workers, standing in the drains on a hot day with pints in their hands. Sid Shepherd was a good worker and played a major part in the building of the village hall.

The building secretary and architect was a local resident, Mr D Drummond, who worked for Durham County Water Board. Local quarries donated materials such as sand and, to save money, second-hand bricks were used – but these needed to be cleaned. One ex-resident, Sheila Wilson, remembers as a child of 11–12 years old:

It took several years to build the village hall, entirely by voluntary labour of the villagers
[Gwen Robson]

I remember sitting on the site where the village hall is now and we used to sit in a ring and chip all the old plaster off the bricks.

The hall was officially opened by Mr Ralph M Allison and was followed by a tea and social evening. The *Advertiser* reported that 'Tribute was paid by every speaker to one table marked "workmen", for at that table sat all the villagers who had given up so much of their spare time for the benefit and enjoyment of their fellows.'

A commemorative stone, still visible today on the wall of the village hall, recognises this achievement by the villagers, simply stating:

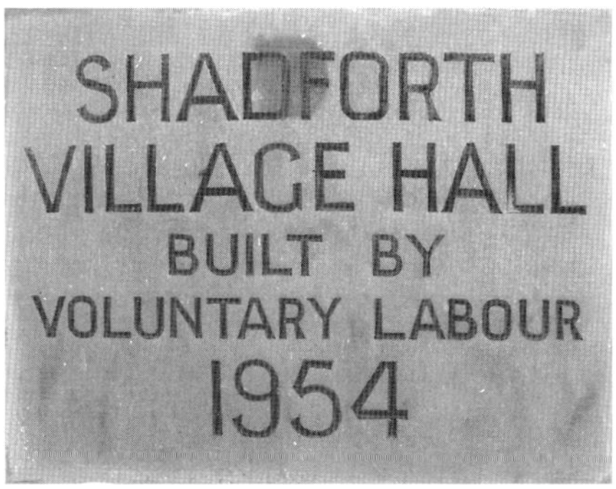

The commemorative stone on the village hall, recognising the effort employed freely by the villagers
[Helen Grindley]

Several sources have said that this stone tablet was once the top of a marble washstand, which was covered in concrete to look like stone and inscribed. One resident at the time also recalls a plaque, on the inside of the village hall, with a list of all the workers who helped to build the hall, but this has not been seen in recent times. Another resident thinks she can remember commemorative mugs being given out.

Older residents remember the village hall being used for Keep Fit, dancing lessons, discussion groups, whist drives and dominoes.

Music for Keep Fit was played on the piano and about ten members took part, but they did not last very long as we started going swimming instead. A couple gave ballroom dancing lessons.

Leek shows were held in the lounge of The Plough until the village hall was built and then they transferred to the village hall, as it was bigger. Leek shows were a big thing every year.

One resident reminisced:

Leek shows were held in the village hall, but organised by The Plough. They were the best shows in the county because they had a big hall to show the leeks. You had to live in Shadforth and be a member of the Leek Club or grow your leeks in a member's garden to enter the show. Jimmy Simpson, who never showed leeks himself, would stamp the leeks six weeks before showing, to identify the owner. The stamp made pin pricks on the leeks. Prizes in the late 1950s and 1960s were a tea set or set of pans.

Flowers were also included in the show, as another competitor recalls:

We used to try and vie with Freddie Ollett – he won a lot – he was such a good flower grower. The show was every September and lasted all weekend. Everything was benched by lunchtime Saturday and then judged behind closed doors. Doors opened again six o'clock Saturday night and you'd go and look. Sunday night, everything was raffled. There were cups and shields as prizes. I've sat many a day with a big, rust coloured chrysanthemum with a yellow centre, turning out the petals – they had to be perfect spheres.

One lady recalls:

The village hall was used for wedding receptions and concerts, whist drives and leek shows. My husband won a bottle of Portuguese wine as a consolation prize in a leek show in 1954. It was donated by Mrs Watson and would have been for a 'special' as they called it, maybe for the best leek in show. They used to give vouchers as prizes too in the 1950s and you could buy coffee tables with them.

More than fifty years later, this lady still has the bottle of Portuguese wine unopened!

The Women's Institute was probably the main user of the village hall. Local residents would use the hall for wedding receptions, and one person can remember ice cream being served at the end of one occasion, appearing on trays from the ice cream factory across the road.

The village hall is an example of the determination, resourcefulness and community spirit that existed and, we believe, still exists, in Shadforth.

A Christmas party in the village hall in the 1970s
[Jean Ord]

In 2002–03, the village hall was modernised and redecorated with a grant from the National Lottery Fund. It now has access for wheelchair users, a hearing loop, modern kitchen and toilet facilities and central heating.

The hall is very well used on a regular basis, providing a venue for clubs and social activities. None of this would be possible without the dedication of the members of the Shadforth Community Association. This Association, which was the driving force behind the building of the village hall, was started by a group of residents, including Mr E Davis and Mr S Sanger. As Sheila Wilson recalls:

They formed a committee and every house in the village was visited to see if they would become members. I can remember Dad and I going round every house ... getting people to pay annual subscriptions, we did it for years ... I used to tear the little receipts out. Subscriptions were maybe 1s 6d – it wasn't a great deal but, if everyone in the village joined in, it was quite a nice sum coming in.

These subscriptions are still collected by the Association on an annual basis and most households are happy to contribute.

SHADFORTH
COMMUNITY ASSOCIATION
*
CONSTITUTION
AND
RULES
*
NOVEMBER,
1952

Mr Walton's original copy of the Shadforth Community Association Constitution and Rules from 1952
[Helen Grindley]

A book, *Constitutions and Rules*, was produced in November 1952 for the Shadforth Community Association, setting out the rules and regulations. The objectives of the Association were:

a *To promote the well-being of the residents of Shadforth by providing facilities for the cultural and social welfare of all age groups.*
b *To foster a community spirit for the achievement of the above object and for such other objects as may by law be deemed to be charitable.*
c *To maintain and manage the Shadforth Village Hall in furtherance of all or any of the above principles.*

The Association shall be non-political and non-sectarian.

In 2004, Shadforth History Group staged an exhibition to celebrate the fiftieth anniversary, or Golden Jubilee, of the Village Hall. Old photographs and 1950s memorabilia were on show, together with quotes from people who remembered building the village hall fifty years previously.

The exhibition in the village hall
[Helen Grindley]

The village green

The village green is a major feature of Shadforth. The green runs in an east–west direction, with a single row of houses on either side, each house possessing a strip of land and referred to as a 'toft', 'garth' or 'croft'. Shadforth is mentioned in *Local History Publication No. 12* (1977) by Brian Roberts, entitled *The Green Villages of County Durham*. In the book, he states that village settlements in Durham 'are dominated by the well known "green villages", ie, those settlements which cluster around an area of open grassy ground set aside, in the words of a recent report, for the "playing of lawful games" and grazing certain animals.'

Shadforth is described as an average sized settlement. For villages to become established and be successful, they had to 'provide enough arable land, meadowland, grazing land, timber for building, underwood and peat for fuel, as well as a stream to drive a mill.'

Access to water was an absolute necessity for village settlements and Shadforth had springs around the village as well as Shadforth Beck. Village settlements tend to favour good drainage, such as outcrops of sandstone or magnesian limestone, and Shadforth lies within the magnesian limestone belt.

Roberts suggests, in his publication, that, 'The green originated as special and enclosed grazing land, close to the houses, part of the dwelling area where beasts could be collected, sorted, protected during troubled times, where the house-cow could be tethered, where communal activities, games and festivities could take place, and where specialist services, the water supply, the smithy, the ale house, the pound, and the common oven could be sited ... There were no grounds for seeing green villages as defensive military structures but they were defensible in times of need and must have often had gated entrances.'

Ezra Smith on the village green in the 1960s
[David Smith]

The village green in the 1900s
[Elaine Avery]

In more modern times, there is photographic evidence of cattle grazing on the village green, possibly en route to milking. One farmer remembers cutting the grass on the green:

Shortly after I started work in 1935, I used to cut the village green at least once during the summer each year with the horse reaper. No other village greens were cut in those days – I had always been obsessed with tidying up the village throughout my adult life. I eventually cut the grass right down to Paradise both sides every year until I retired. I always claimed that Shadforth started at Paradise.

The trees on the village green are relatively modern and some people would say they visually enhance the green. However, older residents remember when there were no trees on the village green and some strongly objected to them being planted:

At one time there were no trees on the village green. A man planted three trees outside my house, I don't know what type, but I said, 'You're wasting your time, before you get home they will be out!' and I hauled them out. The trees get too big and they stop up all the drains.

Many people remember the village green as a place for playing children's games, in particular football, cricket, quoits, netball, rounders and boxing. Some of these games took place as part of school sports days.

There were no trees on the village green in the 1930s. Some time between 1935–1939, two very big street lamps were erected with greenish lights. One was put on the big green, opposite Long's Farm House (West Farm). It lit up the 'Top End' wonderfully and children were allowed to play out 'in the dark'. The other light was somewhere near the top of Oliver Crescent. But, in 1939, the War came and the blackout was enforced. The telephone kiosk arrived in about 1938–9. The grass on the big green was kept short, possibly due to constant treading by 'free-for-all' games of football and cricket and 'serious'

The village green in the 1960s
[Elaine Avery]

quoits. The smaller green, outside Brown's Buildings, was often long and it may have been cut with a scythe to make hay – nothing was wasted. Many folks kept rabbits (not as pets!), so they collected dandelion leaves.

One man had good reason for remembering his football days:

You got caned if you broke windows playing football and you'd get a good hiding from your parents as well. Pigs' bladders were used for footballs.

The Church Lads' Brigade would march on the village green and below is a photograph of them boxing on the green during a sports day.

below **Extract from the** *Shadforth Parish Magazine* **of 1920**

Sports day on the village green. Albert Yard (standing, left) **in a boxing contest, 1946**
[Phyl Yard]

C.L.B. Cadets and the Training Corps.

We hope all parents will read this because we are anxious to know what they think about the C.L.B. and its aims and purposes. The C.L.B. Cadets is an organization for older lads from the ages of 14 to 19, and no lad is allowed to become a member until he is 14 years of age. The Training Corps is for the younger lads of our parish, aged from 10 to 14 years. There is also a Scouting Section connected with the T.C. We want recruits for C.L.B. Parents, do you wish your lads to be helped in the fight against Sin and the World and the Devil ? Do you want them to live Christlike lives ? Then send them to the C.L.B. and T.C. and don't take them away if you have lads in already.

Games of marbles, hitchie-dabber (hopscotch), tops and whips, chasie, blockie (hide and seek) and skipping were also played, but in Shadforth the favourite game was 'jumping the beck'.

Often, children walked over the three fields and back the lane way, picking flowers with friends just for something to do. Otherwise, there was jumping over the Beck by the old smithy and daring to go under the low bridge near 1 North Side, by Grandma York's, without getting feet wet! 'Hitchie-Dabber' (what was hopscotch?) was played, traced out in the dirt roads or chalked on hard surfaces, and 'Two-baller' bouncing balls off a wall to set patterns. There was skipping together in a long rope to rhymes, telling who had to join in the rope or leave it next, and so on. And, of course, 'Tops and Whips', with chalk patterns on them – all had their seasons! Boys (never girls) played marbles. Both played 'Blockie' (Hide and Seek) and 'Chasie'.

With my friend, Winnie, I spent a lot of happy hours jumping around in the farm loft at Dene House or playing with dolls in the kitchen on winter nights – and being given milk and gingerbread before running back up home at bed time.

I remember a piece of thick metal tubing, resting on two crosses of wood, making a barrier to the opening to the fields at the 'Top End'. We did gymnastics on this beam!

On the night of Durham Regatta, children climbed on the toilets ('netties') at the 'Top End' to watch and cheer the fireworks.

I used to do skipping and tops, but my favourite game was jumping the Beck. I remember playing who could jump the farthest or onto the steepest side. Children spent a lot of time playing on the farms.

We used to dam up the Beck and there would be a tree that went over and you would find a rope and we would spend all day in this horrible, muddy pool, with the rope, swinging like Tarzan. Your mams never had to see where you were, they knew where you were, no-one bothered you, no-one molested you. Boys played football and cricket on the village green. We would go up the Dene to play in the summer – ten or twenty kids, with a bottle of water and a few sandwiches.

National celebrations took place on the village green and often included dancing around the maypole, either on the green or up at the Rectory.

I can remember a portable maypole that was put up on the village green for a special occasion. We made patterns with ribbons.

I remember a maypole which was kept in an outhouse at the Rectory. It had a white pole and coloured ribbon.

There was a special sports day on the village green for the Jubilee celebrations in 1935, where races were run and different coloured ribbons – red, white and blue – were given for first, second and third place. Prizes were set out on a trestle table near the present recreation ground and the person with the highest score had first choice. I chose a tennis racket, but there were plenty of prizes for everyone. At school, we had to learn to sing 'Here's a health unto His Majesty' and were all given a mug with a picture of King George V and Queen Mary on it.

I remember the school having a maypole which was put up on the village green during my schooldays. Every child had a partner and mine was the headmaster's daughter who was a lot younger than me. We practised the dances to make the patterns with the ribbons. There were garden parties on the village green where the women all wore fancy hats. A telegraph pole would be taken down in order to have a greasy pole fight and there was also racing.

VE Day in 1945 was celebrated on the village green, with children in fancy dress, and captured for posterity in a photograph.

There was a display of shrapnel at Bourne House, where Mr Oliver, the councillor, lived. Mam and Mrs Winter had teas on in there and Olive Oliver did the baking. The yard was all done out, it was immaculate that day. The Church Lads' Brigade was there playing.

Fancy dress party on the village green, believed to be VE Day celebrations in 1945
[Sheila Wilson]

Residents also remember dressing up for the Coronation of Queen Elizabeth II in 1953.

I was dressed in coloured crepe paper as a rosette. I had white canvas shoes and, because it was so wet, the coloured paper dyed my shoes. They never went back to being white!

The Edwards family dressed up for Coronation Day in 1953 Left to right **Elaine as Elizabeth I, Barry as a Coldstream Guardsman and Avis as a Coronation Rosette** [Avis Clarke]

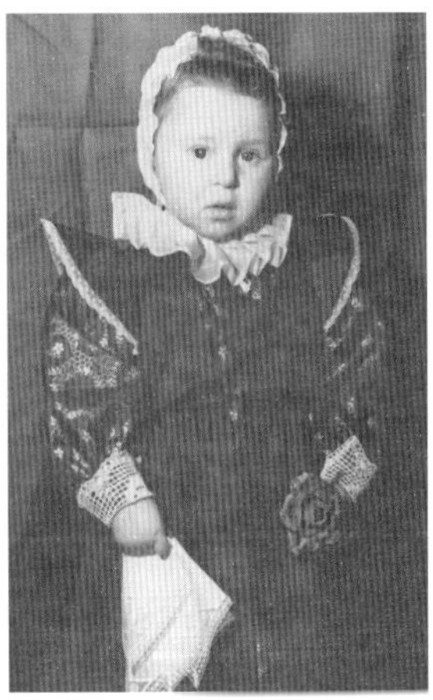

Diane Horrocks as Elizabeth I, on Coronation Day 1953 [Nora Strong]

'Ashville', North Side, decorated for Coronation Day 1953. [Avis Clarke]

Children growing up in the 1980s also remember the village green:

One of the memorable things about our childhood in Shadforth was the get-togethers on the village green. Summer fetes seemed a grand event, with races up and down the green (there were fewer trees then and the grass was flatter), lots of stalls and children's fancy dress competitions, with a large number of entrants. There always seemed to be a good turn out. Though there was always a chance of rain, we remember it always being sunny! At other times, the green was also the centre for congregation. There was an Easter Bonnet competition at the Spring Fair. The wedding of Charles and Diana on 29 July 1981 was particularly special, as we had the day off school! We remember watching the wedding on TV and joining the party outside where people sat at a long table, enjoying party food. There was bunting and general cheerfulness.

It was enjoyable to grow up in Shadforth with the countryside to enjoy, walking and cycling along the lane (avoiding combine harvesters, etcetera!), swimming in the Beck, playing on the bales, collecting conkers, blackberrying and sledging in the Dene in winter. There seemed a greater variety of wild flowers and wildlife in the old hedgerows, which have reduced over time. The park was fun and, although it had perhaps less swings than others, it did have

Elaine Edwards as Gypsy Rose Lee and Avis Edwards as a knitting bag, at one of the church fete fancy dress competitions in the 1950s
[Avis Clarke]

A fancy dress party on the village green in the 1960s
[Elaine Avery]

Judging the Easter Bonnet competition at the village fete in 1979
[Ian Thompson]

a stream and a tunnel under the road to explore. One year, there was the excitement of a summer youth club in the village hall, with the creation of pottery animals and a trip to see 'Raiders of the Lost Ark'. The hall had a toddler group and Christmas parties where we remember seeing a magician.

On Halloween, groups of us would dress up and go halloweening. Bonfire night was always special, with a bonfire in the park (necessitating a bonfire watch to stop people from neighbouring villages setting it alight early) and fireworks. The church and graveyard was full of mystery and colourful flowers. We liked looking at the gravestones to see who was buried in the graveyard. We must have had a sense of 'history', even at an early age. The green was a great resource, as we could ride our bikes around it and play ball games on it (avoiding grumpy residents and cars). One person (who shall remain nameless) fell out of one of the older trees on the green and had to be rushed to Accident and Emergency on an old door, surviving to tell the tale. Near Christmas, Santa Claus even came to visit, riding around the village green on a magical lit up carriage (the back of a truck!)

In the year 2000, daffodil bulbs were planted on parts of the village green, grass verges and entrances to the village to celebrate the millennium.

above **Bulb planting on the village green in 2000**
[Stuart Watt]

The last big, national event to take place on the village green was the Queen Elizabeth's Golden Jubilee celebrations of 2002, with side shows and children's games, including a tug-of-war.

below **A tug-of-war competition for the Queen's Jubilee celebrations in 2002**
[Stuart Watt]

Over recent years, the volume of traffic has increased, the edges of the village green have eroded and, in 2005, a major refurbishment took place. The edges of the green are now protected, the tracks have been resurfaced and the old seats replaced.

The village green in 2005 [Helen Grindley]

Bill Errington left **and Gordon Gilson** right [Stuart Watt]

Shadforth village school

The National School was built in 1863–4. Prior to this, there was an endowed school for girls on the same site, which can be seen on the 1856 Ordnance Survey map of Shadforth.

Information about the school has been obtained from a number of sources: four school logs and School Governors' and Managers' minutes from the County Record Office in Durham, a college thesis from the mid-1960s by Elaine Edwards and people's personal memories.

The college thesis describes a plan to establish a school in Shadforth under a Trust Deed, dated 14th June 1862, when Reverend Blenkinsopp was the first rector of Shadforth. The building was small, one room, a porch and a cottage attached to house the headmaster. It is not known when the school opened, as the first entry in the school log, dated 29th January 1866, states:

The school has been closed since Sept 8th 1865. 19 on the roll, the majority of whom had been in attendance at the school previously.

The first headmaster was Mr Matthew Barron. Lessons consisted of 'the three Rs' – reading, writing and arithmetic – and great emphasis was placed on bible studies, as this was a church school. Clergymen came to the school at least twice a week and, on 8th February 1866, the school received eighteen new bibles. When Mr Barron left, in July 1866, it was fifteen months before another headteacher was appointed.

Shadforth in 1964, with the school building on the right
[Harold Henderson]

Punctuality was very important. Late scholars were punished by making them stand during bible lessons or, as the school log entry for the 19th May 1870 informs us:

Punished those who came late in the morning by keeping them behind the others at dinner time. Great improvement in punctuality in the afternoon.

Another example of punishment written in the school log of 1879 was:

George Musset played truant going after the hounds. He was punished the next day by learning spellings at play time.

Eighteen months later, George was expelled for repeated disobedience.

In 1872, lesson styles were changing. There was a 'gallery lesson' on 'The Potato' and more subjects were being included, such as geography.

Emphasis was placed on needlework and new songs had to be learnt. The school inspection of 1873 stated:

. . . at least 12 songs must be mastered by the children during the year or the grant would be reduced.

The funding for the school was determined by an annual inspection of the standard subjects, reading, handwriting, spelling and arithmetic, as well as needlework and singing. The inspector would complete a government schedule, awarding marks for each scholar. In 1874, the report was poor, leading to a decrease in the grant:

A deduction of one tenth has been made from the grant for faults on instruction especially in arithmetic and spelling.

The system was, in effect, 'payment by results'.

At this time, all work was done on slates but, in 1875, the top class was allowed to write on paper. Ink was obviously being used in 1881, as the school log recalls:

School frightfully cold – ink frozen.

It is recorded that slates were still being used in 1903, but one lady remembers the Infants using slates beyond 1935.

The style of teaching was changing again in the 1890s, with visual aids being introduced. There were pictures for 'object lessons', such as beaks of birds, feet of birds, the ostrich, the elephant and the camel. There were scientific

The pupils and teachers of Shadforth School in around 1893
[Mabel Smith]

lessons on 'melting and dissolving' and history lessons with biographies. The number of scholars was increasing at this time to fifty and the school reports were excellent. In 1898, the report stated:

The work of this little school is really excellent. Besides thought and intelligence in the answers, the very high proportion of the children who answered well in each group was a very striking feature of the inspection. The written work was as 'finished' as the oral. The singing was altogether pleasant and the tone of the school admirable.

In 1893, the original classroom was enlarged and another classroom built of brick to give a separate Infants' class. Both classrooms had galleries, raised platforms so that children seated at the back were at a higher level than the rest of the class. There is mention in 1903 that:

Mr Wood commenced to teach the children military drill on Tuesday afternoon.

The title of the school changed in 1907, as the school log for 8th March reads:

The Board of Education notify their decision to substitute 'Church of England' for 'National'.

The pupils and a teacher of Shadforth School in the 1900s
[Mabel Smith / Bill Errington]

In 1911, the main room could accommodate 81 pupils and the infant class 35, a total of 116.

Ill health and disease are often mentioned in the school logs. On 24th October 1916:

Health visitor visited school and found two children to be in a verminous condition. If no improvement the children will have to be excluded.

A month later:

Mumps has broken out in the village.

In 1918, the school was closed on and off during outbreaks of the influenza epidemics. In 1919, the school was closed by order of the Medical Officer from 20th January to 10th March, due to the influenza epidemic. A week after the school was reopened, the log states:

School opened, attendance poor, many of the younger children being ill with whooping cough. The floors of the rooms have been well scrubbed during last week and the school disinfected.

Disease was still prevalent in 1920, starting with ringworm, one case of scarlet fever and three cases of measles. School attendance dropped to 63.3% and, by 5th July 1920, the school log states:

Shadforth School in the 1920s, with headteacher Tom Brown, who stayed with the school for twenty-five years
back row, left to right
Tommy Weatherall, Ernest Bell, Sidney Gilson, Edward Boardman, Robbie Vest
middle row, left to right
Molly Whittingham, Phyllis Tate, Olive Oliver, Bessie Atkinson, Nancy Fall
front row, left to right
Alfie Plant and Hughie York
[Mabel Smith]

Instruction has been received from School Medical Officer to close the school for 2 weeks owing to the prevalence of measles.

One lady recalled an old fashioned remedy:

If children caught whooping cough they were sometimes taken to the limestone quarry at Running Waters to inhale the fumes from the kilns.

Fluctuation in the numbers attending school often occurred. In 1919, the headmistress informed the Authority she was short of desks and, at one point in 1922, 127 pupils were registered in the school where the maximum had been set at 116. Then, as the college thesis describes:

...a change came quickly. Aware of gross overcrowding in the village and also of the poor condition of much of the property, the Rural District Council took action to remedy this state of affairs and most of the larger families had to find homes elsewhere. Consequently in April 1923 there were only 97 on the register and as time went on condemned houses were demolished with a resultant steady decline in the number of children attending the school.

There is a mention in the school log of a 'Labour Examination' which was taken by twelve year old children which, if they passed, allowed them to leave school for employment, instead of staying until they were thirteen or fourteen years old.

On February 2nd 1920, Mr Thomas Brown began his duties as Head Teacher, staying for a remarkable twenty-five years. Many changes occurred in his time and he is still remembered by older residents. At this time, married women were not allowed to teach in school, so it is somewhat surprising that, in 1924, Mrs Lambton of Shincliffe, who was highly recommended by the Rector of Shincliffe, was accepted as a *temporary* assistant, as there were no other applicants.

During the 1920s and 30s, many improvements and the modernisation of the school took place. Between 1921 and 1923, a new stove was installed in the main room and a new fire in the Infants' Room. The water supply was connected to the regular village supply. Prior to this, rain water was collected in a cistern. Electricity was installed in 1927. In the Manager's Meeting of 1926, tenders were sought for installing electric light and a social was held to raise money to relieve the church of this bill. The following year, the local education authority would not help with the installation costs but said it *may* help with the bills from time to time. Although the School Meals Service did not come into operation until September 1943, there was a Meals Act which came into force in 1921 and 1926, when there were strikes at the local collieries. As the college thesis describes:

...on April 28th 1921, for the first time, the Meals Act was put into operation, thus authorising the County Council to allocate a fixed sum per meal for the provision of food for the scholars affected. Fuel and all services were provided voluntarily by the villagers. Meals were served in a large shed loaned for the purpose which had been thoroughly cleaned. On the first day 52 children had breakfast and 63 had lunch. This service lasted 10 weeks. In 1926 the Meals Act was in force for 23 weeks.

During this time too, it seems the school and the village were coming together more. The entry in the school log for 23rd Dec 1920 reads:

School closes for Christmas holiday. In the afternoon, the 1st Class children acted a little play entitled 'King Winter'. Infants contributed action songs and the girls country dances. Parents present.

In 1925, there was a big Christmas party in the school, where the children found:

...gaily bedecked tables laden with food willingly supplied by people in the village.

This was followed by games, dancing and plays in which every child took part.

The Meals Act came into force, providing food for children affected by the miners' strikes of 1921 and 1926

back row, left to right **(unidentified), Charlie Kendle, Bertie York and Tom Brown**

front row **Lisa Harper, (unidentified),** ? **Lisa Lincoln**

[Elaine Avery]

men, left to right **Charlie Kendle, Bertie York, (two unidentified), Tom Brown**

women, left to right ? **Lisa Lincoln, Ida York, (three unidentified), Mrs Cowley, Lisa Harper, Mrs Whittingham**

[Elaine Avery]

A school trip to Redcar
[Elaine Avery]

Outings were organised, as recorded in the school log in 1924:

26 children from Class I plus six older scholars paid a visit to Durham Castle, a tutor of University College acting as guide.

An annual outing to the seaside became established, which included parents, younger children and friends. In June 1937, the trip, on a Saturday, was to Redcar and was attended by nearly all the children from the school.

Schools were reorganised in 1931, following the Hadow Report, which meant that the pupils over the age of eleven were transferred to Ludworth and that Shadforth School could only have Juniors and Infants.

Special holidays and national celebrations are often mentioned in the school logs. One of the earliest was on 29th May 1876, which was Royal Oak Day and the children were given a half-day holiday. Entries during the First World War years included the celebration of Empire Day in 1917, when:

...children assembled on the village green and sang national songs and saluted the flag.

In 1918, the school was closed for three days' holiday, after the signing of the Armistice. On 18th July 1919, every child was presented with a mug by the Peace Celebration Committee and a special week's holiday was given. On 6th May 1935, there was a school holiday to celebrate the Royal Silver Jubilee of their Majesties King George V and Queen Mary, and on 12th May 1937, another holiday for the Coronation of their Majesties King George VI and Queen Elizabeth. On 20th November 1947, the school was closed all day on the occasion of the wedding of HRH Princess Elizabeth.

Mr Brown, the headteacher, is still remembered by former pupils from the 1930s to 40s. He was described as 'very strict' and corporal punishment in those days was quite normal.

Mr Charnock mentions his school days in his *Shadforth, Ludworth and Sherburn Hill Community News* article:

I had been to three schools before the one in Shadforth, two in Lancashire and the one in Ludworth. Shadforth appeared to be far more advanced than the others. Mr Brown placed me in Standard 2, where I would have been had I started there. When I was given simple £ s d subtractions, I could not do them as I had never seen them before. He was a very good teacher but a bit too strict at times. He had a 'tickler' to help him. After we left school at 14 years we all respected him and still called him 'Sir' long afterwards.

Other residents remember:

Mr Brown said to me, 'We're going to fall out, you and me.' But I had had the cane four times already that day, so I thought we had already fallen out!

Mr Brown used to get the stick out and the school mistress used to give the ruler across the back of the knuckles. I got the biggest hiding of my life through my cousin. I don't know what it was about now, but I remember getting a good hiding.

Mr Brown was very strict, yet in spite of all the caning and missile throwing, I failed the eleven plus, no bother!

I used to get wrong many a time for going down to the stream at playtime where children jumped the Beck. You couldn't hear the school whistle down there.

One day I stayed off school to help my mother and the next day Mr Brown said, 'What was the matter with you yesterday?' I replied, 'Please Sir, I had a bad stomach.' Mr Brown said, 'Well, your sister said you were off helping your mam to wash.' I got reprimanded for lying!

In the 1930s, one father objected to his daughter receiving corporal punishment and he took his daughter out of school for a time while the situation was being resolved.

Some memories were happier:

Mr Brown gave me a book, 'A Tale of Two Cities'. I must have been in his good books that day, as he had his favourites.

Folk-dancing by school children at a garden party at the Rectory
[Elaine Avery]

One of my favourite activities was drawing and painting. I spent hours painting friezes for the walls to please Mr Brown.

Being a Church of England School, scripture was very important. Reverend Tillard came once or twice a week.

Every day there was hymn singing and other songs, unaccompanied, the note being given by Mr Brown using a tuning fork. We had some percussion instruments and charts to learn the value of the notes. Colours denoted when each instrument had to join in and beat out the right rhythm.

Happy memories of dancing and nature walks could be recalled in the 1930s:

Every Friday, the last hour was devoted to country dancing with Miss Nesbitt using a gramophone. I loved this, especially if I was given the right partner. Miss Nesbitt did the choosing, however! We were taught a lot of set country dances and once, eight of us went to the Bluecoat School in Durham for a competition. We were also taught a Maypole dance on the village green for a special, national occasion.

Every Spring we planted bulbs in pots with paper caps on to keep them dark. We planted seeds in three or four plots in the school garden every year. We went on nature walks two or three times a year ... drawing hazel catkins.

Most children attending school came from Shadforth, but a few were from further afield. Mr Charnock writes further in his *Community News* article:

Shadforth school also catered for pupils from Old Cassop and Running Waters. These people had to stay all day at school as they would not get home and back in time. The more fortunate ones would bring their meal in a satchel and eat it near the school fire or stove, of which there were two in the big room. The less fortunate would have little or no food at all. There were no school meals then. In winter, when school finished at 3.30 pm, it was dark when they arrived home after walking across the fields.

Other pupils from the school also recall:

I came home at lunchtime, there were no school dinners in those days. Some children would walk to Shadforth School from Old Cassop, across the fields in snow and in the dark. They would have breakfast and nothing more until teatime when they went home.

School milk was introduced in 1934–5. Little bottles of pasteurised (never heard the word before) milk were delivered in a crate, for all! They had cardboard lids with a little hole for a straw in the middle. A real straw too, not plastic. There were lots of spills when pressing out the holes.

During the Second World War, school life was sometimes disrupted. The entry for 1st September 1939 reads:

National Emergency – School has been closed for a week. All is in readiness to receive evacuated school children from Newcastle upon Tyne.

On Sunday 10th September 1939:

19 children have been received into Shadforth as evacuees from Sunderland.

However, on 18th September:

The eight junior children evacuated from Sunderland and pupils at St Joseph RC School are absent today because managers at their school refuse to allow them to attend until they can be assured the RC children will be in the absolute charge of their own teacher.

During these difficult times, the children were praised for their behaviour, as the entry for 10th October:

An air-raid warning was sounded about seven minutes to two, the 'all clear' signal being given at 3.15. The children behaved splendidly.

The school was used twice in 1939 for Air Raid Precaution instruction and the next year plans for an air-raid shelter for forty-four people were drawn up.

The pupils of Shadforth School in 1946
[Sheila Wilson]

Examination of the children's respirators was documented in the school log.

In 1941, Dr MacMahon called at the school to immunise eleven children against diphtheria. In the same year, a boy ran out of the playground and was knocked down by a cyclist, cutting his leg. In 1943, midday meals started to be served at school, with fourteen of the twenty-seven children having free meals, the others paying 6d a meal.

Mr Brown left the school on 31st January 1945, after twenty-five years' service, and an era came to an end. Throughout his time at Shadforth, the school received glowing reports from the inspector.

Miss Annie Farnworth took over as head teacher on 1st March 1945. On 5th July 1946, PC Purdie called at the school to examine the bicycles – ten were examined and all found to be faulty.

1946 is remembered for very bad weather that winter, as the entry for 26th February 1947 recalls:

Worst blizzard of the year. I arrived 9.10 having walked from Thornley and Miss Dixon at 9.15 having walked from Sherburn.

Emergency rations of 'steak and kidney pud, meat soup and apricot pud' were given out, as the normal meals could not be delivered.

Pupils of Shadforth School in around 1948, with teachers Miss Annie Farnworth centre left **and Mrs Annette Drummond** centre right
[Sheila Wilson]

Another generation of Shadforth residents remember their school days in the 1940s to 60s. Pupils at this time had very good memories of food, perhaps due to rationing:

There was a cupboard at school with emergency rations. We all wanted to have emergency rations because when the cupboard door opened you could smell the barley sugars. There were two dinner ladies, Mrs Errington and Mrs Peachey. School dinners came in containers. Milk came in little containers, a third of a pint. Sometimes they were frozen cold and would be put beside the fire to thaw out.

Polly Errington was the dinner lady at our school. The dinners used to come in containers but, if it snowed, we had a huge cupboard in the hall with tins of ham. I can remember when the war finished and getting boxes of apples. It was such a treat. The apples were covered in blue tissue which we kept for the loo!

Polly Errington was the school cook. Tables were set up after morning break for lunch and there was lots of washing up afterwards.

On 6th May 1948, the school received a gift parcel from an eleven year old school boy, Keith Rochow, in South Australia. It contained one pound of barley sugars, half a pound of crystallised fruits, two pounds of sugar, one pound of beef dripping, one tin of jam, two tins of camp pie and four jellies. The sweets were distributed and eaten while the other things were left for the school leavers' party in July.

The air raid shelter featured in pupil's memories too:

The village school had outside toilets and an air raid shelter, made of brick with grass growing on the top, two doors at either end. The inside was pitch black, there were no lights. There were brick 'sticky out panels' from floor to ceiling, that's the best way I can describe it. I haven't a clue what they were for. It was not very wide, you couldn't have lain down. You could have sat down, but there were no seats. We played in there at playtime, daring each other to go through. It was dark, damp and spidery.

I got the cane for going in the air raid shelter. It was forbidden.

There are few memories of lessons, but some of playtime, concerts and sport:

I loved school. I can still picture the garden where we had our garden lessons. I can remember concerts at school. We used to build a platform at the end of the hall and put on 'Brer Rabbit plays'. The teachers were Miss Dixon, Miss Farnworth, Miss Alvey and Mrs Drummond.

I can remember sports days on the village green. Girls played rounders and the boys played cricket. In the playground we played 'hitchy-dabbers'. We would fill an old round shoe polish tin with soil to make it heavy, draw lines on the ground with chalk and throw the tin and jump and hop.

We used to skip and play a game called 'mounty kitty'.

Miss Alvey was my first headmistress. She had an old Morris car which she could never get started and the kids had to push it.

Mrs Reveler was a good teacher, very strict. When you passed your eleven plus she would take you to her house in Sherburn where she gave you coffee and biscuits for an hour as a treat.

There was a big hall at the school with two fires, one at each end. When it was wet and cold we had to take our slippers and our shoes were put around the big fire to dry.

The Top Class of Shadforth School in 1957
back row, left to right
David Smith, Michael Fall, John Nicholson
middle row, left to right
Marjorie Smith, Avis Edwards, Christine Laws, Joyce Strong, Gwen Usher
front row, left to right
Barry Edwards and Steven Maughan
[Elaine Avery]

A very sad entry in the school log on 10th October 1946 describes the death the previous evening of a nine year old boy, Thomas Pritchard, killed by a fall of sand in the quarry, whilst on his way to choir practice. People today still recall it vividly:

They had detonated at the quarry that day, but it hadn't gone off. Children used to slide down the quarry face. I was making table runners and centres for a sale of work at a teacher's house when there was a knock on the door to say Thomas had suffocated. It was a real tragedy because we all knew everybody in the village.

They had blasted during the day and they must have left a loose overhang. The kids had been coming down the face where they had blasted and the overhang fetched away. I had the job of getting the doctor because no-one had telephones in those days. I had just got a brand new bike, so they said to me, 'Get away and get the doctor'. All the family were up there trying to get him out. It was a terrible tragedy in a small village.

It was a custom in those days for the eldest boy and girl at the school to take flowers to the funeral. One lady remembers picking flowers for the funeral of Lance Davis:

Lance was 21 and worked at Long's Farm. He had been to Thornley for his lunch and was late getting back. He was on his pushbike and took the turn very wide at the bottom of Paradise Bank and went straight in front of a bus.

The village school in the early 1960s, with headteacher Miss Reveler centre right [Louise McEnaeny]

They took him to Paradise Cottages and then the County Hospital, but he died. Lance was a really lovely man. He used to build bonfires for Guy Fawkes night and a guy for the top. The winters were always bad and he would give children rides on their sledges. He loved wild flowers, so we were taken up the Dene by our teacher to pick a huge bunch of wild flowers for the funeral. It was May.

In 1947, a portable Bush wireless set was delivered to the school, bought with money left for the purpose by the previous head teacher.

Weather again featured in the school log of 11th Feb 1953:

A photograph from a newspaper article describing the campaign to keep the village school from closing
The Northern Echo December 1962
[Ethel Stout]

Heavy wind and snow. The older children took the Infants home. Two live wires collapsed from pylons on to the village green. The village phone was out of order.

In 1953, on 20th November, the school nearly burnt down, as a report in the management meeting reports:

... the boards beneath the stove were found to be burning. Mr Whittingham removed the stove and found wooden piles under the boards were also alight and if left overnight the school would have burnt down.

In 1953, Violet Reveler took over as head on 1st December and remained there until the school closed on 20th March 1964.

The school celebrated its centenary in 1963 with a display of art in the school and a celebration in the village hall, and anyone connected with the school in any way was invited. The children entertained the guests with country dancing and action songs and the atmosphere was described as pleasant and informal. When school closure was first threatened, parents campaigned against it, and there was an article about this in *The Northern Echo* of 4th December 1962.

Despite letters and petitions to the Ministry of Education from numerous people, including Shadforth Social Committee and Mothers' Union, the closure went ahead after Easter in 1964. Falling pupil numbers and the deterioration in the building itself may have contributed to the closure of the school, but Durham County Education Committee wanted to transfer pupils to Sherburn Hill for integration reasons and to ease staffing problems. Officially, it was felt that children benefited from being taught in classes of the same age group and not in a mixed five to eleven year age group, as at Shadforth.

The school building was put up for sale in 1964 and sold to an architect, who converted it into a private house.

The village school closed in 1964. The 'sold' sign can be seen in the window. The school was converted into a house the following year
[Harold Henderson]

St Cuthbert's Church

The Parish Church of Shadforth is dedicated to the Northumbrian saint, Cuthbert, and was consecrated by Edward Maltby, Lord Bishop of Durham, on August 5th 1839. From Norman times, Shadforth had been part of the ancient parish of Pittington and was served by priests from the Church of Saint Laurence in that village.

The building of a new church in Shadforth was prompted by a large increase in the populations of the villages of Shadforth, Sherburn, Sherburn Hill, and Ludworth. New collieries were sunk in these areas, attracting many miners and their families. Shadforth remained an agricultural village, with a population of about 180 in 1801; by 1841, this had risen to about 336. The splitting-up of the ancient parish of Pittington took place formally on 8th May 1841, at a Court held in Council at Buckingham Palace, attended by Queen Victoria herself. The Pittington parish included Pittington, Elemore, Hetton on the Hill, Shadforth, Ludworth and Sherburn. The Court ruled that the whole of Shadforth Township, with Ludworth and most of Sherburn Township, was to be served by the new Church of Saint Cuthbert in Shadforth.

The first incumbent of the new parish was the Reverend R G L Blenkinsopp BD, who had the title of Perpetual Curate. At that time, it was known as the Shadforth Parochial Chapelry, and the 'living' was in the 'gift' of the Dean and Chapter of Durham Cathedral. This meant that the income from land allocated by the Dean and Chapter provided an income for the incumbent. For Shadforth, this was about £260 a year. In order to provide a residence house and offices for the incumbent, the Bishop of Durham and Thomas Hooper of Yorkshire conveyed a parcel of land (2 acres, 2 roods,

St Cuthbert's Church in the 1920s
Johnston postcard [Betty Dodd]

The church in around 1910
[George Nairn]

Clergy serving Saint Cuthbert's Church in Shadforth as incumbents

1839–1876	Richard George Leaton-Blenkinsopp	37 years
1876–1885	Thomas Thornton	9 years
1885–1886	James Henderson	1 year
1886–1915	Willmore Hooper	29 years
1915–1929	Thomas Henry Perkins	14 years
1929–1958	Ralph Henry Tillard	29 years
1958–1967	Alban Prentice	9 years
1967–1981	Cyril Esmond Woolstenholmes	14 years
1981–1986	Edward Morris	5 years
1987–1994	Geoffrey Watson	7 years
1994–1997	Paul Allinson (Curate)	3 years
1997–2003	Penelope Martin	6 years

and 33 perch) to Her Majesty's Commissioners for Building Additional Chapels and Churches. This was built in 1840 by Benjamin Adamson, and the incumbents of Saint Cuthbert's Church lived in that house, later known as the Rectory, until it was sold in 1967.

The status of the parish was altered in 1866, when the Reverend Blenkinsopp was appointed as the first Rector of Shadforth. The living remained in the gift of the Dean and Chapter, but now had a net value of £335. The Rector now had complete control of the glebe land and could sell it, if he so wished. (By way of comparison, the Curate in the Parish had a stipend of £20 per annum! A house in Church Villas was provided for his use.)

The rector also had mineral rights, and there is a record in 1889 of a lease granted by the Reverend Willmore Hooper, the Rector at that time, to the Right Honorable John George, Earl of Durham. The lease, for seven years, allowed this coal owner to bring the Hutton Seam of coal under part of the Shadforth glebe lands, the area being about 2 acres 3 roods and 4 perch. The consideration for this was 4 pence per ton of coals per annum. Later, in 1941, a claim was made for compensation under the 1938 Coal Act, and in 1947 a report was prepared by a consultant mining engineer for damage to the Church by subsidence.

In 2002, a United Parish was formed to include St Laurence's at Pittington, St Mary's at Sherburn, and St Cuthbert's at Shadforth. At the end of 2002, following the resignation of the Reverend Penelope Martin, on health grounds, an arrangement was made to serve the United Parish by a priest with oversight, assisted by three self-sustaining curates.

The 1887 edition of the *Shadforth Parish Magazine* gives a picture of the various services held at St Cuthbert's Church and in the Mission Church in Ludworth. On weekdays, several teaching activities took place, as well as more social gatherings.

	Sunday
8 am	Holy Communion
10.30 am	Morning Prayer, Litany and Sermon
12 noon	on the 1st Sunday of the month ... Holy Communion
2.30 pm	on the 2nd Sunday ... Service for Children
3 pm	at Ludworth, except on the 2nd Sunday ... Evening Prayer with address
5.45 pm	Holy Baptism and Churchings, and at any time by giving notice to the Sexton. There is no fee for Baptism
6.30 pm	Evening Prayer with Sermon
	Wednesday
7 pm	Evening Prayer and Address, and on the greater Holy Days
	Weekday Meetings
Communicants' Class	Thursday before the First Sunday in the month, 7.30 pm in the Rectory
Teachers' Meeting	Monday before the First Sunday in the month, 7.30 pm in the Rectory
Young Men's Class	Sunday, 2 pm at the Church
Temperance Society	Every alternate Thursday, 7 pm, Girls' School Room, Sherburn Hill
Band of Hope	Every third Thursday, 6 pm, Girls' School Room, Sherburn Hill. First Friday in the month, 6 pm,
Music Society	Shadforth School
Blanket Club	Tuesday, 7.30 pm, Shadforth School
Library	2 to 2.30 pm, Shadforth Reading Room
Sunday School	6 to 6.30 pm, Shadforth Reading Room
	Shadforth at 10 am and 2 pm. Ludworth at 2.30 pm

Drawing by W. C. Chapman.

St Cuthbert's Church, drawn by W C Chapman
[Betty Dodd]

The *Shadforth Parish Magazine* at that time was priced at one penny per copy. The *Magazine* account for 1887 records that, while the cover was printed by Thomas Caldcleugh in Claypath, an insert was bought from a London publisher for £6 13s 0d per year. The carriage charges to bring this insert from London to Durham, and from Durham to Shadforth, were 12s 6d and 3s 2d respectively per year. Times were bad, however, as not everyone could afford to buy the magazine, and the *Magazine* account accumulated a deficit of £4. So, in January 1889, publication ceased for two years. It was restarted in January 1891, but the former insert 'Home Words' was replaced by 'Dawn of Day', which was cheaper. All seems to have gone well until August 1893, when a deficit of £2 caused another gap in publication until January 1894.

Restoration of the church

Consideration was given to the restoration of the church in 1887, but it was considered prudent to build a parish room first. The reason for this concerned the location of the Sunday School while any work was carried out on the church. Furthermore, if services were to be held in either Sherburn Hill Girls' School or Shadforth School for six months or so, there was a distinct possibility that the congregation would dwindle almost to nothing. So, at the public meeting held on 24th February at Sherburn Hill, it was decided unanimously that it was desirable that the parish room be built. A committee

above, left and right **Inside the church**
[Betty Dodd]

left **The interior of St Cuthbert's Church in around 1910**
[George Nairn]

was formed, subscriptions invited, and notice was given that a grand concert, in aid of the Parish Room Fund, would be given by members of the University and their friends in Durham Town Hall on the following Shrove Tuesday.

Within a month, however, there was an occurrence of some kind which led to the parish room plan being postponed, at least for some months. At the vestry meeting in April 1887, it was decided that the church must be restored, and Mr Hicks of Newcastle was to be asked to prepare the plans and specifications. The Grand Concert, now in aid of the Church Restoration

The church interior
[Betty Dodd]

Fund, was given in the Town Hall in June by several ladies and gentlemen, including the Choir Master of Newcastle Cathedral, as well as members of University College and a Minor Canon of Durham Cathedral. The concert was said to be of the best, 'but the attendance was very thin in the back seats', the sum raised being only £6 8s 6p.

The fund increased slowly over the next year or two, standing at £540 by August 1888. A comment was made that, out of 81 subscribers, 74 were non-residents, and nearly all had never even seen the parish of Shadforth – another indication of the hard times being experienced by the people of Shadforth. Hard times too, for the Earl of Durham, who stopped making his annual subscription of £10 to Shadforth Parish Church.

There is no record of the Restoration Fund progress for two years, as publication of the church magazine was discontinued. It was restarted in January 1891, when it was reported that the restoration of the church was progressing well. Also, the intention to replace the existing bells with a 'sweet bell of 5 cwt 1 qr 6lbs' was taken, to be made by Messrs Taylor's famous foundry at Loughborough. The new bell was used for the first time on Ascension Day in 1891, its 'sweet tone giving the greatest satisfaction'.

The restoration of the church was finally completed, and the re-opening took place on 22nd July 1891. Unfortunately, on the day, there was heavy rain from morning until late at night. The proceedings began with a luncheon for the Lord Bishop and others, held in the Rectory. Then the opening service of Evensong took place at 3 pm, at which the Bishop preached a 'powerful sermon' on the greatness of the English Church. It had been intended to follow the service with tea in the Rectory grounds (price 9d) but, because of the rain, this had to be held in a marquée and there were three 'sittings-down'. The Lord Bishop was far from well and unable to join the congregation at tea, so he had to be driven directly from the church to Durham. At 7.30 pm, a second Evensong was said, the preacher this time being the Archdeacon of Durham. The choir wore newly acquired cassocks and surplices on both occasions.

There is a gap in the story of the church, as magazines have not been located, except for a miscellaneous collection from 1944 to 1951. There are some personal recollections, however, which are of interest:

You didn't have to go to church, but it was encouraged. If you went to Sunday Children's Eucharist at 11 am, you were given a 'stamp book' for sticking in the appropriate picture stamp each week. The rector, Mr Tillard (better known to some as Ralph Henry), gave out the stamps at the end of the service. This was a proper, shortened version of the Communion Service and taken very seriously, but only the Rector and his sister, the organist, took the bread and wine. If you were absent one Sunday, you had to explain the reason and ask for a 'sick stamp' with 'Reasonable Let or Hindered' printed on it. For one full book you were given a medal with one angel, then two angels, three angels and so on, gaining a book of prizes for every three years. I received an encyclopaedia first, then the book *No Surrender* about Shackleton, the explorer.

On Ascension Thursday, the children marched from the school to the church in pairs for a service. After it, on the Rectory lawn, a tin full of sweets was scattered by the Rector and we scrambled for them and went home for a day's holiday!

Reverend Tillard must have had 'private means', as he and his sister, the organist, kept at least a cook, a maid and a gardener. He also ran a Morris Oxford car, occasionally used for emergencies, like taking people to hospital.

There was a pageant to celebrate the centenary of Shadforth Church in the summer, 1939. Girls dressed up as ravens with black hoods and wings and danced to music on the Rectory lawn to represent the birds being fed by St Cuthbert. Miss Winnie Whittingham was responsible for this early dance drama!

If you missed choir practice or church, there would be a knock on your door. 'Where was your boy, why wasn't he at church or choir practice?' It was 'high church', with incense burning. There were Sunday school trips. We had a trip to Durham Cathedral, we hired a big boat from Brown's boatyard and all the choir would be in there, then you were taken round the castle. It was a treat for being in the choir.

School children always went to church on Ascension Thursday for a special service. The vicar used to take us up to his front garden, where he would throw sweets to us and we would dive and catch them.

Canon Tillard would come and ask: 'Have you made your Easter Duty?' He was a lovely man. They used to have sewing circles up at the Rectory and a yearly fête. The next rector, Mr Prentice, used to have a BBQ in the field at the back of the Rectory.

A Sunday School Stamp Album, used by Susan Yard in 1960–61

[Phyl Yard]

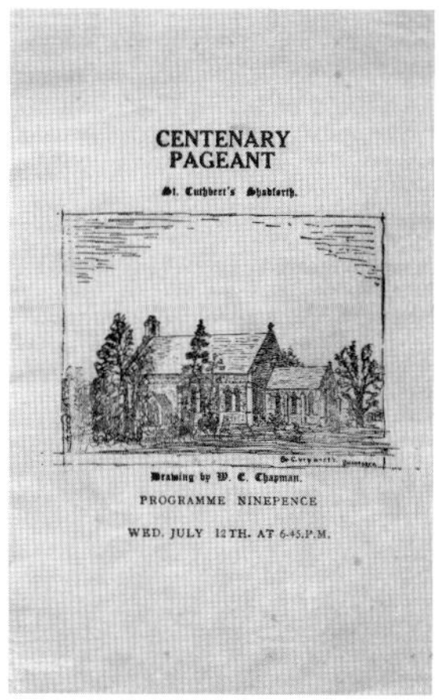

The programme of St Cuthbert's Church Centenary Pageant, 1939

[John Hunter]

St Cuthbert's Church Choir above **in 1936**
[Nora Strong]
right **in the 1970s**
[Fred Blanch]

The Rectory, built in 1839
[Betty Dodd]

A party in the grounds of the Rectory
[Elaine Avery]

above left **The Reverend Ralph Henry Tillard and his sister, Miss Tillard** [Mabel Smith]

above right **Sunday School** [Elaine Avery]

When the Reverend Tillard came to Shadforth in 1928 with his sister, who was the organist, they were very 'high church' and soon introduced the use of servers and the practice of swinging incense. This did not go down well with some of the regular church-goers and they just gave up attending. Also, before they came, several ladies with good voices sang and practised with the male choir. This was not approved of or encouraged by the Tillards.

I can remember Canon Tillard coming to the school on Thursdays to take scripture lessons. As I got older, I went to church on Sunday morning, chapel on Sunday afternoon and Salvation Army on Sunday night. There was nothing else to do.

I can remember wearing Easter bonnets – straw hats. We had gone to Sunday School and we must have been so proud of them, we kept taking them off to look at them. Reverend Tillard told us off saying, 'Either put them on or take them off!'

On the site where the village hall now stands, there was originally a Presbyterian chapel, which later became a Methodist chapel. One resident remembers:

I can remember the chapel on the site where the village hall now stands. Old Charlie Kendle used to preach there sometimes. I belonged to the Girls' Friendly Society, led by Winnie Whittingham. It was a bit like the Girl Guides.

Scouts, Guides and Brownies

There were many organisations that people could join, including Scouts, Brownies, Guides, Church Lads' Brigade, Mothers' Union and Girls' Friendly Society, some of which were associated with the church. These organisations suited some, but not everyone, as some people recall:

Tommy Johnson was the scout master, but I only lasted two weeks in the troop.

I was a member of the Brownies. Betty Dodd was Brown Owl. I don't remember camping, but we used to go tracking across the fields in Shadforth.

I was in the Brownies with Eva Dodd and Betty Hope. We used to go up the Dene and have camp fires and sing-songs, but didn't stay overnight.

above left **Mothers' Union**
[Derek Lax]

left **Shadforth Brownies outside the Rectory in the early 1950s**
[Betty Dodd]

above **Shadforth Guides 1949–50**
[Betty Dodd]

1st Shadforth Scouts in the early 1940s
[Betty Dodd / Sheila Wilson]

Tom Johnson, retired Group Scoutmaster, wrote the following pair of articles for the *Shadforth, Ludworth and Sherburn Hill Community News* in 1992, describing the history of Shadforth Boy Scout Group.

The early history of the 1st Shadforth St Cuthbert's Boy Scout Group

In the year 1920, the parish priest at that time, The Reverend T H Perkins, as sponsor, authorised his curate, Reverend A R Stobbs, to become the founder of the first Shadforth Boy Scout Group.

The following is an extract taken from the March 1921 edition of the parish magazine.

'The Troop of Scouts and the Pack of Wolf Cubs are going along famously. A large increase of members has taken place since Christmas. There are now thirty-seven lads in the Scouts, ten from Shadforth, thirteen from Sherburn Hill, and fourteen from Ludworth.

The training is very practical, eg, ambulance, telegraphy, cooking and physical training – the ambulance work has been done splendidly under the charge of ASM Mr Stewart.

The real spirit of Scouting, which is certainly the greatest asset in our work, is gradually being caught by the lads. This is the spirit and atmosphere which will make the movement alive and of long existence in the parish. It creates enthusiasm and keenness without which no organisation can thrive. We are working steadily during the springtime, in preparation for the Camp

1st Shadforth Scouts in the early 1940s
[Betty Dodd / Dorothy Stead]

in August – a delightful country spot amidst the pine trees where the lads can have a real jolly time.

The Wolf Cubs have a membership of eighteen lads from 8 to 12 years of age. Miss M Marley and Miss Simpson are in charge of the cubs. They work hard for stars or badges – very practical work.'

Reverend Perkins also quotes, 'The more I know of the Boy Scout Movement the better I like it, it is really, I believe, the most beneficial of its kind for boys that has ever been started. One of its most extraordinary features is the fact that it is conducted for the good of the boys and not for the headquarters and its officials! Absurd red tape, which is strangling the very life out of so many of our Church Societies and costing great sums of money, is non-existent among the Boy Scouts.'

May it ever remain so!

After the death of Reverend T H Perkins, a new rector was appointed, Canon R H Tillard.

Already, Reverend A R Stobbs had moved on, and the following curates, the Reverends D Hague, S Chapman, C Charlton and G Renwick, acted as Leaders to ensure the movement flourished until the beginning of World War II in 1939.

Throughout this period, the following Leaders gave valuable assistance to the Scout Troop – Mr Steward, A Dodd, H Brown, V Collins, L Atkinson, M Local, R C Smith and J Williamson. Among other helpers, were Bob Allen, Tom Kellett, Leslie Marley and members of the Rover Crew. Miss M Marley, Miss Simpson, Miss B Brown, F Jones and A U Atkinson were responsible for the continuation of the Wolf Cub pack.

1st Shadforth Scouts in the 1950s
[Betty Dodd]

Among the highlights, probably the most outstanding was the awarding of the Group's first King Scout Badge to Scout Jack Williamson – an honour so richly deserved. Later, Jack was appointed Assistant Scoutmaster under the leadership of that gallant and devoted Scoutmaster, Bob Smith.

During these many years of Scouting, there was one very sad occasion for, in June 1929, a most likeable and enthusiastic Scoutmaster, Vincent H Collins, died as the result of an accident in the Sherburn Hill Colliery mine. The death of this prominent leader, greatly admired by all, caused much grief and sorrow, not only in the movement, but to the entire locality. As a tribute to Vincent, six candlesticks, presented by the Group and friends, were dedicated and placed as a memorial on the altar in the parish church.'

More reflections on the 1st Shadforth Boy Scout Group

In 1939, the dark clouds of war began to roll, and it was on 3rd September that war was declared between Great Britain and Germany.

Soon, the young men of the area were being called up to serve in HM Forces. Naturally, like other organisations, the Scout Group found it difficult to find leaders. ASM Jack Williamson had joined the RAF. Jack was the Troop's first King Scout and, unfortunately, lost his life whilst serving in the 1939–45 conflict. A memorial to Jack, a silver wafer box, a gift donated by Scouts and ex-Scouts, was dedicated by Canon R H Tillard. The wafer box is still used each Sunday at the service of Holy Communion.

The Troop languished for a while. Then, in 1942, Mr Tom Johnson offered his services to assist Scoutmaster Rob Smith, and the Group began to reassemble once again. It was rekindled with six young boys who were keen to become Boy Scouts. Soon, it grew and, in a short period, it had a membership of thirty boys.

The Cub Pack, under the leadership of Cubmaster Alan U Atkinson, began to blossom too.

To our delight, the girls of the village reformed the Girl Guides and Brownie sections, under the leadership of Marjorie Blacklock, Betty Hope and Eva Dodd, and progress was made in both numbers and efficiency.

In 1943, the enthusiastic Group Scoutmaster Bob Smith decided to get married. Rhoda, his wife, gave him and the Troop excellent support. However, Bob, who was residing in Durham, decided to begin his association with St Oswald's and hand over the Shadforth Troop to Scoutmaster Tom Johnson.

During the following years, honours came thick and fast to the Troop. The spirit – enthusiasm, keenness and efficiency – reaped its reward. Ten Queen Scouts Badges were gained by the boys of the Troop – at one period, six scouts were awarded their badges en bloc by the late Chief Scout, Lord Rowanham. At that time, it was believed to be a world record for a Troop to receive this unique achievement. Many 1st Class badges were awarded, likewise many 2nd Class badges were earned and, at one period, the Troop adopted six new members, all from the Elemore Hall Residential School – all passed their Tenderfoot badges and were enrolled as Scouts. The membership of the troop was increasing and, as some of the boys were growing older, so it was decided to form a Senior Scout section under the leadership of Rover Scout Bill Humes. Later, on his discharge from the Army, Wilf Dodd became Senior Scoutmaster. The Cub pack was not to be outdone, for they were earning badges too, and were runners up in the Durham and District competition for the totem pole, and a team received miniature cups on winning another event. The Troop also had its success in District competitions, winning the Stopford Shield and the coverted Lonsdale Cup.

Since the formation of the Group in 1920, four of its leaders were awarded the distinction of the Medal of Merit, the first being G S M Bob Smith and he was followed by G S M Tom Johnson. The third was S M Sandy Major and then Cubmaster Alan U Atkinson. Such recognition can rightly be regarded as an honour to the Troop which they have served so long and faithfully.

We also had the tremendous backing of a parents' committee, working and organising events to earn money for new tents, camping equipment and to assist the renovation of the church hall. The efforts of these willing volunteers, under the leadership of Mr Herbert Prichard and Mr Arthur Dodds, was greatly appreciated.

We owed much to our local farmer, the late William Gilchrist of Crime Rigg Farm, for his kindness and assistance in permitting us to use land for our camp training weekends. Our church parades gave a lot of satisfaction to our chaplain, Canon R H Tillard. The Troop also provided choir boys and, later, Sunday School leaders as part of our promise, 'Duty to God'.

Our first adventure of Camping standards took place in Malligill Woods, Leamside. It was Whitsuntide 1943 and, amid glorious sunshine, several of the boys spent an excellent weekend under canvas. This picturesque site holds happy memories for our Scouts and they often remark of the happiness and brotherhood found there.

Quite a number of our members had their baptism of camp life on this lovely site. During this memorable camp, the Troop gained one of its greatest ambitions, that of becoming joint holders of the Stopford Shield.

Farming, mining and rural life

Shadforth has always been considered a farming community. It has never had a coal mine of its own although, at one time, it was surrounded by six local pits and many men who lived in Shadforth worked as miners. Colin Granlund stated that even as late as 1972, mining was the main employment in Shadforth compared to 1987, when there was only one miner. Mining, therefore, did affect village life, as demonstrated by the following sad article found in the book *The Thornley Coal Company owners of Thornley, Ludworth and Wheatley Hill Collieries 1830–1885* by Wheatley Hill History Club.

1st September 1865
2 miners brothers killed in Thornley pit, George and Liddell Wallace. Another man Matthew Hewitson badly burned and later died. Inquest – Accidental Death. Brothers buried at Shadforth. On Sunday last, the funerals of the brothers George and Liddell Wallace took place in the little neat churchyard of Shadforth, in the presence of a very large number of their friends and fellow workman ... Altogether there would not have been less than 1,000 persons present. George Wallace aged 41 – left a wife and 8 children, 3 of them working. Liddell Wallace aged 31 – left a wife and 3 or 4 children, eldest being 7 yr, youngest a baby.

Matthew Hewitson buried on Mon 28th left a wife and 4 children. He had been injured 6 times previously by accidents, some of his fingers had been taken off and his face and other parts of his body were marked through injuries he had sustained.

A large memorial stone erected for the 3 men.

The memorial stone in Shadforth churchyard to the three miners who died in Thornley Pit in 1865
[Helen Grindley]

Everyone in a close knit community like Shadforth would have been affected by a tragedy like this.

The main farms in the village were Dene House Farm, West Farm and Crime Rigg Farm. Dene House Farm has always been associated with the Foord family, who lived there for three generations. West Farm was associated with the Flower and Long families. Crime Rigg Farm is still farmed by the Gilchrist family. Hill House Farm, to the northeast of the village, was associated with the Johnston family, who initially lived at Oxclose Farm to the southeast of Shadforth. The Johnston family originally came from Gateshead, where they had a commercial business. Harry Johnston was able to travel the country, taking photographs which he then produced as postcards, many of which survive today, including some of Shadforth. The Johnston family left Hill House Farm in 2000, but it is still farmed by the present tenants. The cottages at the bottom of the hill, known as Paradise Cottages, were where the farm workers lived at one time. A farm called Low Croft is visible on one of the 19th-century maps, but stone foundations are all that remain today. One

The Johnston family, taken at Oxclose Farm in 1924
[George Nairn]

farmer remembers it being called 'Langleys' and farm machinery being stored in the barn, but no-one lived there. High Croft farm lies further southeast from Low Croft.

Cold Knuckles Farm, to the west of Shadforth, was only accessible across the fields. Mr Gordon Smith remembers living there as a child in the late 1930s and having to walk across the fields during the dark winter months to attend Shadforth School. The Farleys were thought to be the last people to live at Cold Knuckles Farm, after which it was knocked down – a pile of rubble is still there today, marking the spot.

Shadforth Mill, not far from Cold Knuckles Farm, is also a ruin, very little of it remaining to give any indication of its use, apart from the mill race. The Crawfords were the last couple to live there. Mr Crawford died in 1916, but his widow continued to live there until 1925, after which time it became deserted.

Bourne House, or 'Burn House' as it was originally written, was built some time between 1856 and 1897. It was bought by T M Oliver in 1912 from Mr J Burton and, in June 1914, he opened a blacksmith's shop beside the house. He started off farming there with some cows and selling milk. By the latter half of the 20th century, a piggery and chicken farm had been developed by the Shepherds who then owned Bourne House.

The skinnery or tannery to the east of Shadforth is marked on the 1856 map. No-one remembers it as a tannery, but some people still remember the houses that were there, although there is no sign of them now.

The main sources of information about the farms are from retired farmers and the residents of Shadforth who remember their parents or themselves working and playing around the farms. There is also a family diary, belonging

At Cold Knuckles Farm in the late 1930s
above left **Ethel and Gordon Smith**
above right **Mrs Smith and Gordon**
[Gordon Smith]

Cold Knuckles Farm, west of Shadforth, in around 1912
[Betty Dodd]

Hill House Farm in the 1940s
[Frank Johnston]

to the Gilchrist family, started in about 1869 and finished in 1955, which was shown to Shadforth History Group; for which we are very grateful to Mr Edwin Gilchrist. The History Group was also lent a copy of a university thesis by Ursula Patrickson, entitled, 'A Geographical survey of the area embracing Sherburn Hill, Sherburn, Sherburn House and Shadforth in the County of Durham'. This gave some interesting details of the industrial, agricultural and social life of people in the area during the Second World War and we are grateful to Betty Dodd for lending us this thesis.

The present Hill House Farm was built in 1952. The original house occupied a site slightly further down the hill. It suffered badly from subsidence, which became so dangerous that the family had to move out. Although nothing remains of the original house, memories survive:

The house looked like a street, though it was one house. One end was a stable and then four rooms downstairs and upstairs, a back kitchen, pantry and a dairy on the north side, but every window in the house faced south. One cold water tap in the back kitchen provided the water. There was an old-fashioned stove in the kitchen with a water boiler at one side and the oven at the other side. There was a damper which was pulled out to heat the water. The boiler was always full of hot water. Hot water was scooped out the boiler with a tin and mixed with cold water to use, then cold water was added to the boiler to replenish it. In the back kitchen there was a massive boiler which was lit once a week to do the washing. The cooking was done on the fire with a big oven on the side.

far left **Dorothy Stead, John Stead and Kathleen Law visiting Hill House Farm in 1941**
[Dorothy Stead]

left **Dorothy and John Stead** (left)**, Eric Stead and Jean Tate** (centre) **and Kathleen Law and Jenny Lucas** (right) **at Hill House Farm in 1941**
[Dorothy Stead]

In the old house the children used to cycle to the toilet because it was a long way, past the stables, round the orchard and behind the other stable. It was an earth toilet.

The orchard had apple trees and pear trees, but the goat killed the trees because it ate all the bark.

At Oxclose Farm there was a big range with a massive oven which could take about a dozen loaves of bread, sufficient to last the week. The fireplace was so big it would take five scuttles of coal at the back of the fire which were then raked forward a few at the time. The fire never went out.

As for farming itself:

I came into farming towards the end of the agricultural depression in 1935. My father's hired worker, Joe Henderson, was horseman and general farm worker. He lived at Dene House Farm like one of the family. His weekly wage was twenty-six shillings (£1.30) a week, no overtime. Miss Nancy Bewley also lived at Dene House. She helped my mother in the house and milked four cows morning and night for six days a week. I remember the loyalty of these young people for what seemed little reward, yet they were happy and content and kept in touch.

Most of the work was manual in those days. We got our first tractor in 1942. Up till then, Clydesdale and Shire horses were used to plough the fields. They were used in pairs and sometimes threes.

The farm had about thirty dairy cows and the milk was delivered to Thornley, carrying it in urns and using a pint or half-pint measure to dispense it. People came to their doorstep with a jug. There was no pasteurisation, the milk came straight from the cow, but it was cooled. It was cooled in a container by putting cold water down the inside while the milk ran down the outside. There would be approximately twenty-six gallons that had to be sold that day. If any milk was left, it was sent to the Co-op dairy at Wingate. The wagon came and picked it up and that milk would be pasteurised and bottled.

During the Second World War:

There were seven of us working at Hill House Farm at that time and two Italian soldiers helped during the war, although they weren't there very long. The prisoner of war camp was at Coxhoe Hall and the Italians used to cycle to the farm every day to work with the men.

On VE Day I didn't join in the celebrations in Shadforth because I was scuffling potatoes in the field above the park – that is, going up between the rows with a horse-drawn machine to cut the weeds out. The machine was called a scuffler.

I remember VJ Day better. It was harvest time, and I had cut a field of oats the day before and I had to go and stook it. It was a pouring wet day and we had on our macs and wellies (in the early days, we wore boots and leggings), and it was so wet that I had to pour the water out of my wellies. There were six of us stooking that day, all soaked to the skin.

Known as 'The Bright Hour', women from the Wesleyan Methodist Chapel gathered outside Hill House Farm, busy knitting, possibly as part of the war effort in the 1940s
[Dorothy Stead]

Children playing on a horse and cart in Shadforth
[Betty Robinson]

Ursula Patrickson describes a typical farmer in her thesis, written during the Second World War:

'The typical agricultural worker of this neighbourhood has the following characteristics. He is strong, sturdy, reliant, hard working, dogged often in his ways, and possesses great powers of physical endurance. One sees him ploughing in the coldest and most bitter weather and he knows the qualities of his land from A to Z. He is the typical English yeoman of old.'

As her thesis is a geographical survey, Ursula Patrickson also describes different soil types and suitable crops:

'One field may be very dry and limey, owing to the presence of the limestone under the surface soil, and it will be very suitable for certain kinds of crops. The farmer, knowing this, buys his seeds and plants accordingly. Another field may be composed of sandy soil which, I am told by one of the local farmers, is very good for certain classes of potatoes, *eg*, Sharps Express early potatoes and King Edwards potatoes. These potatoes, he told me, do not grow well at all on clay soil, because of the presence of too much moisture. The clay does not allow the rain to filter through the soil, therefore it remains muddy and sticky. I then asked the farmer if potatoes were not grown on clay soil, but he told me they were, a certain type of potato liked clay soil, eg, Duke of York potatoes and Great Scot potatoes. Thus the farmer must know the nature of his land and, as it is very varied in these villages, there is a variety of crops grown, *eg*, a variety of potatoes are planted according to the merits of the various fields.'

Potatoes, turnips, wheat and oats were grown and, during the War, Savoy cabbage. Not much barley was grown, as oats were preferred to feed the stock. During the holidays, school children and women from the village would come and pick the potatoes. One year, when it was difficult to find anyone, women came all the way from Sunderland. One lady remembers picking potatoes, when she was aged nine or ten years old:

It was the week in October when you were off school, all the children would go potato picking on Stan's farm. The farmer had pegs and would stride out, something like eleven strides, and put a peg in, then another eleven strides and a peg, and that was yours. You would go with your bucket, sandwiches and tea – whatever your mother gave you. A machine would go around and hook the top bit off and scatter the potatoes, and you would pick them up and put them in a sack. You would pile them all together and they would come round later and move the sacks. It was hard work, you were filthy, you were jiggered, but it was good fun, apart from when it rained. It was all day from nine o'clock in the morning. The highlight was the lift up the Dene on the back of a trailer on the tractor, wearing your wellies and scarf.

Below Hill House Farm was a row of cottages called Paradise Farm Cottages.

There were four cottages at Paradise in 1935. The two cottages nearest the farm housed the farm labourers, the Godfreys, who had four children, and the Rainbows, who had two children. The two cottages nearest the road were let by the coal board for the villagers. There was a family called Hutchinson, who had four children in a 'one down one up', and the Charnocks, with three children.

One lady remembers living at Paradise Cottages as a child:

There were only two rooms in the cottage. We had a fire in the kitchen, with a boiler at the side. There was a scullery with a washing boiler. The kitchen fireplace was lovely and had to be black leaded. There was a leaden tin to get water out the boiler and you had to be really careful that you didn't spill any, as the fender was polished and mother was very house-proud. We had a sitting room at the side of the kitchen. Upstairs were two bedrooms. My parents had the one above the kitchen and four children slept in the other one. My brother had a single bed in the corner with a clotheshorse around it and we three girls slept in a double bed on the other side.

During the War, we had a big shelter with an iron top and bars around it in the sitting room, which we had to go inside. I remember a bomb dropping at Silent Bank.

My mother used to go out and work in the fields at night with my dad. They would harvest the turnips and were paid two shillings per row, and they were very big rows. As children, we would also go and work on the farm. I would help with the cows, giving out the feed, my dad telling me how much to give them.

This lady's sister also remembers Paradise Cottages:

I was born at Paradise in 1937. My dad was a farmer and head cowman for Johnston's. He used to do all the milking and some ploughing with horses. I remember him chopping turnips for the cows and putting it out with the cow cake. I used to love being on the farm. We had a big vegetable garden and used to keep hens and ducks, rabbits and guinea pigs. Once, when my brother was at Ludworth School, the children were asked, in a scripture lesson, 'What was in the garden at Paradise?' A child replied, 'Godfrey's hens and ducks!'

We had a dog called Lassie. If dad, who smoked a pipe, forgot to take it with him, he would fasten a note to Lassie's collar and send her home to collect it. Mam used to fasten the pipe to her collar and she would take it back. Dad always had a wisp of straw.

During the War, there were soldiers at Ox Close – it was a search light base. Italian prisoners of war dug out the roads in 1942 when they were blocked with snow. They also used to do farm work. Gilson's at Sherburn had Germans working for them. I don't remember any animosity. The prisoners of war used to make toys such as wooden, pecking hens and carved rings out of aeroplane glass. I can remember planes going over and a whistling bomb hit Haswell Plough. We had a shelter in the sitting room, with khaki blankets over the top and sides and mats on the floor inside. My mother made clippie mats and sold them to people in the village.

above **Mary Godfrey feeding the hens at Paradise Cottages in 1950**

[Betty Robinson]

left **Frank Godfrey and his dog Lassie, outslde Paradise Cottages in 1950**

[Betty Robinson]

Mr F Charnock wrote an article in the *Shadforth, Ludworth, Sherburn Hill Community News*, describing his time at Paradise Cottages and the purpose of the windmill below Hill House Farm:

We went to live in Paradise Cottages, Shadforth, in 1922. The farmer at the time was Peter Raine. The mill's purpose was to pump water from the adjacent well for the farm and Paradise Cottages' people, who had to carry their water in buckets. The carrying was done with the aid of a wooden square which kept the water away from the carrier's feet, thus avoiding splashes.

There were no lights anywhere at night. If the mill was broken down because of damaged fins, etc, then the horses were sent down to the beck at Paradise Cottages to drink from the beck. They made their own way back.

We could hear their feet as they went past. Eventually, taps were installed and the mill fell into disuse. I feel it is a pity it was not preserved.

The third house from the left was occupied by a family of nine. There were father, mother and seven of a mixed family in a 'one up and one down', with a little back scullery. The parents slept downstairs, in something called a 'desk bed'.

A farmer remembers a wonderful childhood being brought up on a farm – it was all he ever wanted to do. He remembers, aged about three or four, milking a cow:

The cow had its feet in the pail many a time and whatever I got was given to the cats, 'cause in them days we had cats to keep the rats down. It was done to keep me occupied.

This young farmer was always wanting to help on the farm. When he was a little older, aged nine or ten, he remembers taking the horse and cart to lead turnips in from the field and then backing it into the yard on returning:

I used to turn the horse around and back it into the shed and I thought I was marvellous doing this, but I think the horse could have done it by himself!

The skinnery was situated on the road out to Ludworth. Ursula Patrickson describes the skinnery in her thesis:

'The work was to tan the hides and skins of the animals which were killed. There was no elaborate system of tanning as there is at the present day, the work was very primitive. A stream runs past the 'skinnery' in which they washed the hides with a little lime to loosen the hair or wool. The hair would then be scraped from the skin by some primitive method and washed again. Then it would be tanned by placing it in a container of liquid containing tannin. The tannin would be obtained from the bark of trees, especially oak.'

Peggy Redden, who lived in one of the skinnery cottages, wrote an article in the *SLS Community News* in 1992, which is reproduced here:

There was a tannery (leather works) between Shadforth and Paradise Cottages. When the stream was in flood, the water came into the houses which were situated at the tannery. The water was sometimes four feet up to the inside walls of the cottages, which was about the height of four drawers in the dresser. Everything possible had to be carried upstairs, including coal and water. Sometimes it would last three days, and the paraffin light was used. One lady, who was stranded upstairs, lowered a basket, fastened to a clothes line, from the upstairs window and a man who lived near put bread, etc, into it and the basket was hauled up. Apparently, a newspaper photographer took a photo of this.

The floors were painted with red ochre and, as the flood water came through the house, it was red with the paint. When the flood water went down, there was still some water left in the round coal oven, and it had to be ladled out before the oven could be used.

The beck ran underneath the houses through an arch. If the 'peg' was put in before the flood arrived, it held the water back and prevented it from coming into the yard. When it was dry, you were able to walk through the tunnel to the other side.

There were four houses with a coal house each, but only two toilets.

The beck was eventually diverted, to join up with Paradise Beck, which helped to reduce the flooding.

There was also a windpump sited just east of the village near the beck.

Mr Charnock remembers the photograph mentioned above:

I remember that being taken by an official photographer who could have been from either *The Northern Echo* or the *Durham Advertiser*. I can recall it because it was during a flood. One school chum who was with us was wading in it during our dinner hour. The water at that time was opposite the gate leading to the windmill and, just as the photo was snapped, he slipped into the water.

No-one living in Shadforth at present can remember the skinnery in working operation, but many people have memories of the area flooding:

There were four houses, with water running underneath them and, every time there was a storm, they all flooded. When the houses flooded, the people used to be stranded upstairs and the children would come out in the bathtub to escape, rowing away from the house.

Peggy Redden used to live in one of the cottages. When the skinnery flooded, we used to see people walking on two chairs to get out the cottages without getting wet. It never stopped the children getting to school, because they could go up through the farmer's fields.

Thomas Oliver lived at Bourne House Farm. He started off as a colliery blacksmith and then bought Bourne House, which had a blacksmith's shop. He bought two cows and used to carry the milk around the village in cans. He was a well remembered character:

He used to farm in his bowler hat and pin-striped trousers and he also delivered the milk dressed like that. He kept his farm immaculate – he did not like

The former blacksmith's workshop, at Bourne House
[Edna Wood]

to have a speck of dirt on anything – every last bit of straw had to be picked up. If the cattle made a mess outside, it had to be cleaned up.

Thomas Oliver was a county councillor and had control of the council houses; he would only let houses on condition that the tenants worked the garden. He was a member of the National Farmworkers' Union and used to go to London once a month. He received an MBE at Buckingham Palace on 9th November 1954. He was one of the authors of *The Gilchrist Diaries*, which give a fascinating insight into life in Shadforth over nearly one hundred years. Entries include everything – matters of farming; council or parish business; recordings of births, deaths and marriages; work going on in the mines; the weather; the price of produce; national events; or just a simple note about nature. Here is a selection, written as they were scribbled down, without particular attention to grammar or punctuation.

Extracts from *The Gilchrist Diaries*

1879. The wettest summer ever known it rained every day in the Hay harvest; it turned out a very fine back end for the corn harvest. Crops of all sorts very poor, trade was at its very worst this year. Thousands of men out of work. Pits and iron works laid in. Things took a turn at the back end of the year in 1879 for the better. Very fine Christmas Day also New Year Day 1880.

Sunday School Centenary held at the East End of Sherburn July 10 1880. 1200 Scholars beside Teachers. it was a glorious Day. happiest Day i ever spent among scholars. Sherburn Hill Brass Band attended. The singen went of well. The speaking was good addressed by D D Cook Rev T Rodgers, G Barker and T Eliven G Parkinson Chairman.

March 4, 1882. The mildest winter ever nown never once a show of snow up till the present little or no rain. January & Febuary quite warm. Several birds nests found in January also a sortment of flowers. Febuary the Roads quite Duste

June 16 1883. 192 Children killed at Sunderland in the Victoria Hall with a over crush down stairs and a Bolt in the Door.

March 1 and 2 1886. Greatest snow storm I remember. All Railways and Roads all stoped. It snowed 48 hours. Several men lost in the storm. It cost the country about 100,000 pounds to clear it a way. It took three Day to clear the wagon way.

Coronation day Tea for the children & old people given at Shadforth. Total cost 49-19-1 taken out of the rates. June 22 1911 very windy day tent blown down.

New Year's day 1913 a very fine day almost like spring. Many daisies and buttercups in full bloom.

Dec 16/14 Hartlepool, Whitby & Scarbrough bombardment by the Germans. Many lives lost & wounded, & a great deal of damage to property.

May 5/45 Victory Day. War with Germany finished. 2 days holiday.

June 11/48 Sherburn Hill Pit explosion 4 men killed.

June 10/54 T M Oliver received the MBE in the birthday honours list.

Dec 29/54 This is the finest day have had for months, as I write these notes I can see hay still out & corn still to be harvested, this has been the wettest year I can remember. There will be no regrets at its passing, it has been a bad year for farming land very wet & little wheat sown. Some potatoes still to lift.

Oct /55 Being a grand harvest time, never a stop & good crops. Never remember a better time.

One interesting calculation was included in the back of the diary:

Rule how to mesher a Pig
Square the girt and then
multiply by the lenth and
then Divide Bye 7344
if any remains Multiply
by 14 and that will give
the Pounds Divide by the
above

In the latter half of the 20th century, Bourne House had a pig farm. One young child remembers it well:

There was the piggery at the bottom of our garden and I used to feed the little ones. There was also a big black pipe, a sewer pipe, between our garden and the piggery. A wooden bridge was built between the garden and the piggery so they could move the pigs, but we used to dare each other to balance and walk across the pipe. The pigs were still there when I got married in 1976.

Mr F Charnock recounts again, in his *SLS Community News* article:

The one person who stands out in my mind was the village blacksmith, 'under the spreading chestnut tree', the tree being at Bourne House Farm, until recently famous for pig breeding. His name was old Tom Peacock. Tom was also a cowman and general farm worker. He used to take the cows to pasture behind Paradise and bring them back for afternoon milking. Tom did the milking of course in winter time, he started work by candle light and finished

Samuel Wade and blacksmith Tom Peacock at the smithy in Bourne House
[Brenda Jameson]

in the late evening. He was up at the crack of dawn each day. There were no days off . . .

Farming changed a lot in the latter part of the 20th century. For example, in the 1940s, Hill House Farm had 5 men working three hundred acres, but by 1987 it had two men working five hundred acres. The nineteen farms in 1921 had amalgamated into 7 farms by 1987 and were run like a family business, with labour and equipment being hired as required. One farmer recalls:

We went down to four men and then down to just two at the finish. We used to spend all day long in the tractor or combine on our own. Radios were put in the tractors but I couldn't stand the radio. I enjoyed the old days with the horse and plough, but it was too slow and you had to move with the times.

Another farmer, from Dene House Farm, recounts:

I could not see any future for dairy farming, owing to the unsuitability of the layout of the land at Dene House – with no land adjoining the farmstead. Yet I was determined to break with tradition, as the native Shorthorn dairy cows had been bred to extinction through the ignorance of past Shorthorn breed societies where coat colour was considered more important than economic milk production. I remember hand milking my father's so-called Shorthorns as a schoolboy. There was more milk in a coconut than in some of those Shorthorn cows!

Such was the state of agriculture in 1935. This was organic milk of course, but could we afford it? In the late 1940s some English dairy farmers made for the Annan dairy auctions in Scotland to buy attested Ayrshire heifers. I was determined to farm the sought-after black and white British Friesian heifers that originated from Holland and South Africa, because of their exceptional milking ability and strong constitution. There were only seven herds in the county at that time. I yearned for an agricultural college education in dairy farming, because high-yielding dairy cows called for rather special feed and management know-how. However, it hadn't to be!

These black and white Friesian cows were bred into an award-winning herd by Stan Foord, topping the Durham County National Milk Records for four consecutive years, between 1957 and 1960 inclusive.

Many children remember the cows being milked and the milk being delivered:

As a child, I used to go and see the calves at Stan's farm. I used to watch the cows come and go into their own space in the byre. The cows used to go up the Dene, past Whittingham's house, along the track rather than the road. They all knew the way, Stan didn't have to lead them; he was at the back, stopping the cars and they all stopped, no-one tried to get past them, they just waited. I can picture the man who used to milk them, he let you stand

Dene House Farm, with the South Durham Hunt in around 1908. It is now two separate houses, The Shutters and Dene House

[Stan Foord / George Nairn]

and watch. He had boards above each one, like children's blackboards. He used to have the name of the cow on there in chalk and signs – possibly to do with how many pints they had given.

I never remember anything lying around Stan's farm and he was always dressed dapper – even after a day in the fields.

At four to five years old, I remember milk deliveries from a horse and trap which had a little door on it. My uncle used to take it out with another lad called Ivan Smith – he had ginger hair. They would open the door and ladle out the milk into a jug. Soon after that milk was delivered in bottles. At Stan's farm, milk came straight from the cow. It was warm and had to be cooled before going into the churn.

On 11th October 1978, the first of two sales of the Dene House Farm British Friesian Dairy Cows attracted over eight hundred pedigree breeders from all over the United Kingdom, some buyers flying in by helicopter. It achieved the second highest priced sale average per cow in the UK at that time. The top cow (Denehouse Lonely 9th RM. RMX. RML. Excellent) sold for six thousand guineas. In farming terms, Shadforth's finest hour! Twenty-nine cows went to Scotland, forty-two to England and six to the Isle of Man. The previous year, on 15th April 1977, eight heifers were exported to Algeria, flown in from Stansted Airport.

The second sale was in September 1986 and saw the end of Dene House as a working farm.

Children of the 1980s remember:

The seasons were well reflected in the fields surrounding Shadforth, in the ploughing, sowing and harvesting of the crops. Occasionally, cattle were led up and down the green, not always under control, to their fields, leaving cowpats as reminders along the road. At the other end of the village, at Dene House Farm, the black and white Friesian cows seemed very big to us as small children, as we peered in at the door of the 'magical' milking parlour! Twice a day, the herd of cows would troop into the shed for milking by the milking machines. Occasionally, calves were also present. Sadly, the milking parlour and other buildings were turned into houses in the late 1990s, further reducing the village's connection with farming.

Mining was referred to at the beginning of this chapter and miners are often associated with allotments. Ursula Patrickson describes allotments and the use of waste land in her thesis:

Miners Billy Bage and Joe Smith in around 1930
[Joyce St Julien]

Land used for allotments and poultry schemes

Gardening is a very favourite hobby of the miner and, after his hard 'shift' is through, one often sees him enjoying an hour or two digging in his garden. Many of the colliery houses are not equipped with gardens, so pieces of land have been allotted by the Parish Councils and turned into allotment gardens by the miners. The produce of these allotments is amazing and rare specimens of potatoes, carrots, leeks and other vegetables are shown at the village competitions. Some of these allotments present a beautiful display of colour in summer with the different varieties of flowers. The miner can supply much of his own home produce from his garden, eg, garden vegetables, jam and jellies from his fruit trees. Many of the miners make a good deal of money by selling tomatoes from their greenhouses, buckets of flowers and buttonholes and home-grown vegetables. With his profits the miner buys his seeds and plants for next year's crops.

If it is a large allotment, part of it may be taken up by a poultry house, thus the owner has his own egg supply. Before the War, I was sorry to see many of the local allotments unoccupied and full of weeds. This was not only a waste of good soil, but it was a source of destruction to the other allotment holders, for weeds from the neglected gardens were spread to occupied allotments. Since the advent of War, practically every allotment is now occupied and in this area the miners really are trying to increase the supply of home produce.

Certain waste-land has been given to the method of poultry rearing. In these villages there are unemployed and the poultry schemes have become a source of employment and profit to these unemployed men. One hen house and a small patch of land was given to each man, as well as a number of chickens. It was only an experiment but it has been very successful. Its rewards have been two-fold: a) it has been a source of labour and profit for unemployed men (men sell their eggs and hens and buy new chickens) and b) it has put some waste-land to a useful purpose.

The Crawfords lived at Shadforth Mill. One lady remembers:

I was very friendly with one of the Crawford's daughters, Violet, who lived at Shadforth Mill. People used to come down from Sherburn Hill to picnic there. Shadforth Dene was a beauty spot, also used for picnics. There was a pond and marigolds, milk maids, white anemones and blue bells.

The Stead family in Shadforth Dene in the 1930s
[Dorothy Stead]

Shadforth Mill, west of Shadforth in around 1910.
There is little evidence of it today, apart from the mill race
[Betty Dodd /Bill Errington]

Walking around the Shadforth countryside was a popular pastime and was celebrated in verse. This anonymous poem was found by David Smith among his mother's possessions.

A canny walk

You can talk and tell of where you've been,
But have you walked through 'Shadforth Dene'
Past Seldom Seen and Never Seen,
Then along the village green,
Up to the Witey Lonhen, Running Waters, The Three Horse Shoes –
That's where I've been! It's a canny walk!

I've walked from there down the fields,
Across the beck to Blackburn's Field.
Onward past Cold Knuckles and the old Mill,
Up to the well of Sherburn Hill
Then across the moors to Sherburn Hill,
It's a canny walk.

Shadforth Dene in the 1930s. The Dene looks very similar today
Johnston postcard [Bill Errington]

'Seldom Seen' and 'Never Seen' referred to two cottages tucked around the back of the houses on South Side and, therefore, not often seen. One lady, who moved to Shadforth in 1946, remembers living in one of these houses and still has the rent book for 2 South View:

There were two houses on the front, but we were round the back and looked at nothing. Next door was the Whittingham's house and their yard and on the other side was another house, but we looked at nothing and that's why it was called 'Seldom Seen'. The house only had two rooms, a living room and a bedroom, though the bedroom was a decent size – no upstairs. There was a boiler and we bought a little oven which we put in the pantry, but there was a coal oven attached to the fire. We got furniture with dockets and points. There was no bathroom, so the water was heated in the boiler and we had a tin bath in front of the fire. There was a flush toilet, but it was outside and froze up every winter. What we didn't know was that water came in round the back, off the fields and through the garden. I used to say we were the only people in Shadforth who could lie in bed and wash our feet at the same time!

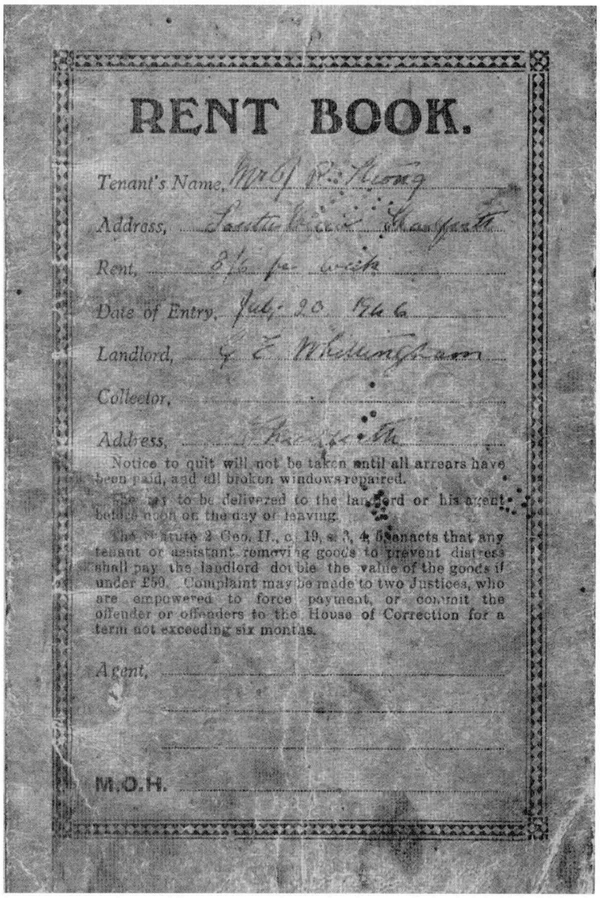
RENT BOOK.

Tenant's Name,

Address,

Rent,

Date of Entry,

Landlord,

Collector,

Address,

Notice to quit will not be taken until all arrears have been paid, and all broken windows repaired.

The [illegible] to be delivered to the landlord or his agent before noon on the day of leaving.

The [illegible] 2 Geo. II., c. 19, s. 3, 4, 5 enacts that any tenant or assistant removing goods to prevent distress shall pay the landlord double the value of the goods if under £50. Complaint may be made to two Justices, who are empowered to force payment, or commit the offender or offenders to the House of Correction for a term not exceeding six months.

Agent,

M.O.H.

The rent book for 2 South View

[Nora Strong]

This chapter ends with an unusual but true story, written by Bill Wood.

When the elephant (nearly) came to town

About forty-five years ago, I was walking over a field between Witch Hill and Strawberry Farm, near Signing Bank on the main Durham road, when Frank Long hailed me. At that time, he was working Strawberry Farm as well as West Farm, on South Side, in the village. He lived in West Farm, just opposite me on the other side of the green, since the house at Strawberry was quite ruinous.

'Ye've nivver had a look round Strawberry, hev ye, Bill?' he said.

'No, I haven't,' I replied.

'Right then,' he said, 'Howay wi' me and Ah'll show tha' summat.'

With that, he led me through the old farmhouse and around the outbuildings. One of them had been a small smithy with a furnace and an anvil. He told me it hadn't been used for years, and it certainly looked like it, as there was a thick layer of dust everywhere and the furnace still contained the remains of ashes from the last fire. Nearby stood a strong stone barn. He pointed to it.

'See that? Dis thou knaa' we once had an elephant in there?'

I laughed and said, 'Get away with you.' But he was serious.

'When Ah was a young lad, me father had this farm afore me. One day, a circus was travelling down Signing Bank on its way to Durham. The owner came and asked me father if he could rest the animals in their cages on our land, to feed and water them for a couple of days. Me father agreed a price and their hosses pulled the cages off the road for the two neets. It was great to see aal them animals. Mind, they were aal safely locked up in their cages.'

'Well, that's amazing,' I said.

'Aye, but that's not aal,' he continued. 'There was an elephant that had been leading the circus alang the road with its trainer. It didn't hev a cage, so they had to shelter it in that barn. So there, noo.'

He told me that people came up from the village to have a look, and I had to smile when he also mentioned that a couple of fellows, obviously good gardeners, brought wheelbarrows with them to collect the elephant dung!

I reckon that the above incident must have happened in the early 1920s.

A farmer's memories *Stan Foord*

These four articles from *Shadforth, Ludworth and Sherburn Hill Community News* have been kept separate from the other chapters and are reproduced here with just a few minor editing adjustments. Stan has written them well and they seem to flow so nicely. Although three generations of Stan's family have lived and farmed at Shadforth, his grand-parents originated from the Picton area of North Yorkshire. They farmed or managed a small hill farm before coming to the tiny fifty-acre Running Waters East Farm in about 1855, where they also worked the adjoining limestone quarry. Joseph Foord, born in 1714, was famous for devising a unique method of supplying drinking water to farms and villages on the North Yorkshire Moors, constructing seventy miles of water races in his lifetime. In 1915, Stan's grandfather, John Foord, retired to 1 North Side, Shadforth, the same year that his father, Fred, took tenancy of Dene House Farm. Stan was born in Shadforth and has lived here all his life. These articles are not just about farming, but relate to all aspects of village life, as well as showing some of Stan's personal feelings. We thank Stan for letting us print his memories in this book and for his contribution to the village over many years.

Stan Foord in 2004, standing outside the back of Dene House, Shadforth, where he farmed all his life

[Stuart Watt]

Local farmer recalls 'the good old days'

***SLS News* 4** December 1992

My earliest memories of village life go back to around the time of the General Strike – the mid to late 'twenties. This was a period of poverty and despair. I can vaguely remember the school children being offered soup or broth and a bun. The soup was prepared and cooked in the old joiner's shop at the rear of the Plough Inn.

Men stood around at street corners with nothing to do but watch and wait. Some relieved their boredom by seeking firewood from the Dene. Others played quoits on the green for small bets while others looked on. I think it was about this time that they formed a football team. Yet it may surprise some young people that handball was probably the most popular game played by men in those times; all they needed was a gable and a ball.

Yet, in spite of all the gloom and doom, the village green was never short of a few boisterous lads playing cricket or football and it was a poor week if we didn't put a ball through someone's window. The ball was usually retained until repair to the window was paid for.

There was some considerable anti-social behaviour on and around the village green in those days. Thankfully, we now have a playground for the young people to work off their energy. Some boys would chase around after booler hoops, pushing them along with a stick. For others, it would be tops and whips or marbles. The girls played hopscotch and skipping. There wasn't any pocket money in those days. Occasionally, we were given tuppence (old currency) for admission to the little old cinema at Sherburn Hill but, in the main, we lived a simple but healthy outdoor life.

I eventually joined the church boys choir, as did most of the village boys. On Tuesday and Thursday evenings, we used to practise our singing with the rector's sister, Miss Tillard. As young boys we found the Good Friday service, which lasted for three hours from 12 noon to 3 pm, somewhat trying. The church was stripped bare and the hymns and whole service were so mournful and depressing. Easter Sunday, of course, was quite the reverse. The early morning service, at 7.30 am on Ascension Thursday, was a special treat, as the whole choir of about twenty-five men and boys were invited to the old vicarage for breakfast. We had a good gallop around the large, beautifully kept garden and a buzz in the sunhouse. Mrs Browning was the resident cook and housekeeper in those days. She lived in the annexe to the vicarage with her son, David, who was the same age as myself.

Bill Errington, aged 93
[Stuart Watt]

Shadforth vicarage is a delightful place on a gentle southern slope. It is a perfect sun-trap and quite sheltered from the north and east by mature beech trees. The part-time gardener was a Mr Waddie from Wheatley Hill. They don't make gardeners like Waddie any more. He retired when Reverend Tillard (later Canon Tillard) left, having been gardener nearly thirty years. Miss Emily Blenkinsop, the daughter of the very first vicar of St Cuthbert's Church to reside there from 1836, was still living down in the village next to the school. Miss Emily took the bible class on Sunday afternoons for young men. Mr Bill Errington, who still lives in the village, was one of the last to attend her classes. I can still remember her, in her shawl, as she visited my mother regularly in the evenings. My sister would have to take her home and attend to her little jobs: bringing in the coal and lighting her oil lamps. Most houses smelt of paraffin oil in those days. It used to amaze me that there weren't more fires.

Miss Blenkinsop used to buy a railway truck load of coal of twenty-one tons for less than thirty pounds. My father used to haul it from the colliery depot with horses and carts to her huge coal house. During the winter, Miss Emily gave quite a lot of coal away to people in need of warmth. She was a kind, caring lady.

Neither miners nor farmers were at all paid well in those days. In about 1931, coal and potatoes were selling wholesale for around the same price, approximately £1 12s (or £1.60) per ton.

I can remember the miners coming home from Thornley Pit across our fields in their pit clothes with knee pads and helmets, with faces as black as coal; the whites of their eyes showed up whiter than white. There were no pithead baths in those days. Their Colliery Band used to practise together and they would play hymns in Shadforth Dene on warm Sunday evenings. Lots of people came and picnicked with their families and sang along. One of Baldasera's smart pony ice cream floats would come into the Dene at the Thornley end on its way home, if there was any ice cream left.

From 1920, Mr Tom Brown was the Headmaster of the little Church of England village school for more than twenty years. He taught the three 'Rs' and a lot of discipline and certainly didn't need the advice of a child psychologist on how to do it. The cane was like the nuclear deterrent, always a constant threat. Unfortunately, he didn't have much success as far as I was concerned, but that was no reflection on his ability as a teacher. He reckoned that my mind was always up in the turnip fields or mucking out the byre. I couldn't disagree with that. He was an excellent teacher and he taught right from wrong; something that is sadly missing in too many homes and schools today. In fairness to teachers, however, the first five years are the crucial ones for behavioural correction and that primarily is the parent's responsibility. Mr Brown was ably assisted by the home-bred infant teacher, Miss Eva Whittingham. Every Thursday morning, the Reverend Tillard, or our curate, Mr Charlton, taught the Scriptures at the school.

In the 1920s, the Shadforth Farmers and Tradesmens Ball, held in the little village school, was a very special social event for the Shadforth people and the surrounding area. I can just remember names like Aly Smith and Hilda Blanch helping to provide the supper. Willie Gilchrist walked across the field from Cold Knuckles Farm with a hurricane lamp. There weren't even street lights in those days and hand torches were an extravagance. The little school was packed and, if the noise was anything to go by, they were having fun.

In about 1927–8, the first electricity was brought to Shadforth via poles and overhead wires. The head engineer, a Mr Clark, boarded with my parents during the installation. I can remember him playing dominoes with my father and friends during the long winter nights. He eventually became a life long friend of the family.

About one acre of the so-called 'Windmill Field', on the immediate left as you leave the village going towards Ludworth, had been taken for garden allotments before my time. However, about 1930, this area was taken back by Mr Raine, the farmer of Hill House, as some of the allotments were no longer occupied and consequently became untidy.

The wind-pump near the beck was on this same land and it pumped water from a well up to Hill House Farm to a huge storage tank. It also supplied Oxclose Farm, although it was more often referred to as the 'Windmill', as mentioned earlier.

The water supply to the three other farms in the village for livestock was obtained by hand pumps from wells, in one case, the beck at Bourne House. There was also water pumped from a well in the Plough Inn yard in those days.

At the east end of the village, better known as 'the bottom end', near the old bridge parapet (no longer in use), was the best-known and most used well called the Jubilee Well. None are in use today, although the water is still there, as Shadforth lies so low on a base of gravel and running sand with some freak areas that have given problems in the past where drains have to be deep.

Mr Peter Raine, a well-known Shadforth farmer of Hill House Farm, died in 1934. I can remember, as a boy, watching his coffin being borne on a farm wagon, drawn by his favourite grey mare, followed by mourners to Shadforth

Church. I had never seen this before, nor have I seen it since, and I was very impressed. It seemed a fitting end for a grand old farmer.

I can remember Mr John Smith, known locally as Jack, who was a cartman for Whittinghams the Builders for approximately fifty years, with his black horse and flat cart, before they became motorised. He lived in the house on the site of the village hall, at the east side of the Plough. In the middle, between his house and what was an old chapel, there were double doors; this is where he used to do some butchering in his spare time. He reached the age of eighty-nine years, and his son, Ezra, worked as a stonemason for Whittinghams all his life – nearly sixty years. His two daughters provided the suppers for the Farmers and Tradesmens Ball and his son-in-law, Fred Blanch, was sexton for nearly twenty years after him.

Memories from Shadforth's past

***SLS News* 5** April 1993

In the south-western corner of the village, better known as 'the top end', the Brown Brothers (hence the name Brown Buildings) had their wheelwright and cartwright sheds, but that was slightly before my time.

According to my father, these people were great craftsmen and served farmers and trades people over a wide area. All horse-drawn carts, wagons, traps, etc, or anything in the joinery line, were made and repaired there. Ninety per cent of the transport in those days was provided by horses; consequently, there were vast amounts of horse vehicles to make and repair.

The Whittingham Brothers, Mr George and Mr John Robert, were established builders in Shadforth for far longer than I can remember. John Robert died in 1931. It was about then that George's son, Raymond, married and joined the business, having built the new house ('Burnside') for the newly weds.

Mr George Whittingham and the Reverend R H Tillard were, I believe, the first two people in Shadforth to own a car. Mrs Whittingham was a very keen gardener. She made several attempts at tidying up the village, trying to bring some colour to it with rockeries and such like. Unfortunately, our cows had to pass through the village four times a day for milking and, sadly, she had to give it up during the summers. I wish I could have been more helpful. Had she been attempting it today, I would have helped her gladly. Raymond's only son, George, chose not to follow the family tradition. Instead, he became a doctor, thus ending their long-established stone mason era.

In 1936, Whittinghams built some new private houses opposite the church gates and were looking for buyers. My father was offered one for £280, but declined the offer: he thought they were too expensive. Last Christmas, in 1993, I saw a fire grate with a nice brass fret costing fifteen pounds more than those houses cost new in 1936, owing to inflation!

The old Methodist chapel was still in use in about 1928 but, shortly after that, it was converted into a grocery shop by Mr John Morton. Eventually, it

The Shadforth Farmers' Ball around 1950. This annual event became so large that it had to be held at Sherburn Hill Welfare Hall.

[Harry Brass]

was pulled down, in 1952, to make way for the Shadforth Village Community Centre, completed by voluntary labour in 1954.

Mr Robert Francis Thubron (Senior) and his son Bert were the proprietors of the well-known undertaker, cartwright and joinery business, as well as the licensees of the Plough Inn from well before my time. In 1926, Mr Thubron (Senior) retired and went to live in Garden House, opposite Dene House Farm. Bert then took the tenancy of the Saddle Inn, after the McRoys left in 1927, and the joinery business was carried on in the sheds at the west end of the Saddle Inn. There was also a blacksmith's shop there.

However, Bert retired in 1933, and was the last licensee to serve drinks at the Saddle Inn. He then came to live in the Garden House, where his father had retired before him.

The Saddle Inn was then abandoned and boarded up in 1933 and wasn't occupied for seven years, until the Liddle family came from Sunderland, to avoid the bombing, and restored it as a residence only in 1940. It was more recently lived in by their daughter and family, Mr and Mrs Crow.

In 1926, after the Thubrons left, Mr Bill Fickle came from South Shields to manage the Plough Inn for the Tait Brothers, who were also from that area. Eventually, the Taits took it over themselves. One brother died in 1933 and the other left in 1938. Mr and Mrs J Watson took the tenancy in 1939 for nearly thirty-four years, until they retired in 1972.

The Plough Inn and the Saddle Inn both had stables attached. The Plough Inn had a two-stall stable, where the bar is now located; the stable door was in exactly the same position as the present bar door – the grip marks are still in the concrete pavement outside.

The stables were used by stallions travelling the North East to farms, serving mares during the breeding season – April to July. This was big business in those horsey days, when the horse was the most important animal on the farm and in the town. There was an old saying in those days that if poverty got to the stable it soon got to the house! The groom always walked with his stallion. He would take bed and breakfast at the Plough Inn or Saddle Inn while his horse fed and rested for the night, ready to move on the next day. Just imagine, in a town such as Durham there would be more than eight hundred heavy draught horses and about the same number of light vanners and trap ponies, carting and fetching to the station and shops, as well as public transport. There were no oil tankers needed in those days; and artificial fertiliser, herbicides and pesticides were unheard of – organic food was the only kind. Just imagine the mountains of horse manure, besides the cattle, sheep and pigs.

A well-known character in Shadforth was Frankie Sample. He wouldn't take a full-time job, yet he could butcher a beast on Monday and make a coffin on Tuesday along with the best. But, if he was paid for those jobs, he would be in the Saddle Inn most of the next few days or, if it was frosty weather, he could be ferreting rabbits for the rest of the week. I'm talking about the 1930s, long before myxomatosis.

He poached all his life, but he always shut the gates, he was a sort of a gentleman poacher and always reported anything untoward. Frankie lived most of his life at Warwick Buildings in a small two-roomed, single-storey house at the bottom of the Dene Lane, where The Willows house now stands. I went to school with his youngest daughter, Mary. His house was handy for the fields and he had been known to fill a pillow case with mushrooms and pick up a dozen snared rabbits well before five o'clock on a morning. This was his hobby and beer money.

It was well known that Frankie Sample was given a vicious and very dangerous billy goat from someone at Thornley to butcher, as the previous owner had been badly injured by it. However, Frankie decided to keep it for a bit of fun, he was like that, even though no one ever dare go within the radius of the tether chain but the man Sample himself. At that time, Mr Tom Summers was the caller for the miners on the early shift at 2.30 am. One morning, at that unearthly hour, as Tom Summers rapped on the door next to Sample's house, he saw in the darkness, coming towards him, the dreaded billy goat. Old Tom was of a nervous disposition and fled in panic for the nearest outside earth closet. There were plenty of them vacant at 2.30 am on a cold winter morning. He just beat the billy goat as he slammed the door, but he was too late for the toilet, or so it was said.

He remained a prisoner for five hours, until the owner was sent for, whereupon Tom, without a word, but cold and visibly shaken, just walked away home. It was reported to PC Towns that Sample had let the goat off the tether deliberately; he was then ordered to put it down.

Mr Tom Oliver, Uncle Tom, was farmer and blacksmith at Bourne House. I suppose you could have described him as a gentleman farmer: he always wore his bowler hat, even in the hayfield on the odd occasion when he helped out. He also had a small milk round and delivered the milk himself every morning. He was always well-dressed and his boots were always immaculate but, of course, he never did any dirty work, though he worked as a farmer and blacksmith when he was younger.

He spent a lot of time on various committees. He was one of the promoters of the Milk Marketing Board, and Honorary Member, also Chairman, of the Durham County National Farmers' Union. For very many years, he was Chairman of the Parish Council; though he could be abrasive at times, he was well respected. His faithful old blacksmith, Tom Peacock, was the last to shoe horses and do general repairs to horse-drawn implements at the village smithy. The little old forge, now dilapidated, still stands by the side of the footpath at Bourne House,* where he also milked and tended a few cows.

There were none tougher than old Tom Peacock. As a schoolboy, I sometimes took our farm horses to be shod and Tom had an awful habit of chewing tobacco, like so many men in those days, and he would be spitting everywhere. It was a case of keeping well out of range. I was always relieved to get out unscathed! The cost of having a heavy horse shod all round with new shoes was six shillings and threepence in about 1934.

Mr S Joice, or 'Old Sam' as he was better known, was the village oil man. With his horse, he delivered paraffin-burning oil from a tank on his horse waggon, where he measured the oil from a tap. He delivered to almost every house and outlying farm in the area for lamps and heaters. However, the arrival of electricity to the village was a bad day for him. His wife and daughter, Cissy, minded the grocery and sweet shop and also the post office on the corner, where few, if any, secrets were ever kept about village life. They collected the post from the box in those days in readiness for the collection van, as well as sorting the incoming mail ready for the postman. As a boy, I remember Mrs Joice telling a customer, 'Maud, there's a card for you. Your Bella's coming on Thursday', without batting an eyelid! When the new, red telephone kiosk was first installed, it was possible for them to listen in at the shop; and what do you think! Les Dawson never heard of our post office. At the slightest provocation, Old Sam would appear at the door, horsewhip in hand, followed by his wife and daughter. As boys, many a time we had to make a run for it – fortunately, he wasn't fast. As a family, they were not the most popular in the village, but I must say they were very clean people.

During the early thirties, most farmers and village people, especially miners with allotments, kept pigs for their own use. They were cheaply fed

*The forge has gone, but the stable, now a cottage, is still there.

from garden waste and kitchen scraps, along with a bit of meal. Most villages had their own self-styled butcher or pig killer; such a man was Tom Hutchinson, or 'Hutch the Butch'. He was a frightening figure to youngsters, with his white beard and his hard hat and complement of knives hanging from his blood-stained leather belt.

Someone had to do this kind of work. I would say that old Tom was even more renowned for the shape and size of his unusual little house, which was three cornered, widely known as the 'Corner Cupboard'. It had one small bedroom upstairs and one room down, with a pantry at the pointed end, one door and two windows. The earth closet was forty yards away by the side of Dene Lane, where Tom Summers once sought refuge. This corner house was the last on the south side of the road leading to Ludworth from the village. The house was demolished years ago, but you can still see the area it occupied.

Stan Foord remembers 'the good old days'

***SLS News* 7** December 1993

One of the two small sweet shops was occupied by Mrs 'Bella' Ferguson, a widow, her son Arthur (who was a school-friend of mine) and her sister, Miss Mary Dodd. I often called there for my pennyworth of marzipan teacakes as I cycled to my 'finishing School' at Ludworth. Actually, they weren't shops as such, just a small house window with a sloping display board. Arthur's mother eventually married Ottiwell York, a well-known Shadforth man from an equally well-known Shadforth family. The interiors of those small houses, (Mrs Ferguson's being one door down from the Corner Cupboard), were a joy to behold, everything shining and clean – and a lovely smell of fresh-baked bread or teacakes as you stepped inside. How did people live so nicely in such small old stone houses, mostly 'happy with their lot', on just a few shillings per week, no 'mod cons', only a cold water supply, and not every house had even a cold water tap? In the main, people seemed to be content with their way of life and one thing they would feel certain about – they would walk anywhere at any time of day or night in absolute safety and they didn't need to worry when their children were out of sight.

The other small sweet shop was another old stone house with a window display, two doors west of the Plough Inn and occupied by the Brown family. As you stood at the living room door waiting to be served, the fireplace, the pride and joy of those old homes was immediately in front of you and I well remember the high wood mantel shelf with a band of red velvet, all tassels and bobbles along its edge. The things that intrigued me as a boy were the two magnificent ornamental black horses rearing up towards each other, one at each end of the high mantelpiece. Does that jog anyone's memory? The Browns also sold lamp oil from a shed in the back yard. Mrs Janet Brown's father and brother lived with them as a family unit – something we rarely see today! Their only child, Nancy, another school friend, has lived at Stocksfield all her married life. Mr Jack Brown was the first person in Shadforth to own a motor-cycle and side-car – he unfortunately died in 1943. His wife, Janet, Nancy's mother, lived to the remarkable age of ninety-five. She was one of the most respected persons in the village at that time, as well as the longest living, apart from a Mrs Mary Oliver, who died in 1851 at one hundred and one years of age – Shadforth's only centenarian. We would like to hear from any of her descendants who may read this article.

The skinnery, tannery or leather works – take your pick – was last operated just over a hundred years ago by Mr Richard Earle, known as the fellmonger. Little is known of the process, but a plentiful supply of water must have been essential. The skinnery itself was a large, square, stone building, with a big yard bounded on three sides by a low stone wall; and, at some later date – about one hundred and twenty years ago, it was converted into four dwellings. The beck flowed through the centre of the building via a brick arch. The whole area flooded most winters and, in 1968, an effort was made to overcome this problem. The National Coal Board accepted responsibility for the subsidence, which had increased the problem, and made a major contribution towards raising the level of the highway by 4 feet 8 inches and diverting the beck so that it ran along the north side of the highway instead of the south, this avoiding the necessity for the two small bridges, the parapet of one still to be seen today. It would have been better if the highway level had been raised still further, as the road still floods; no less than seven cars had to be recovered from the water on 15th May of this year, 1993. Re-grading the beck downstream would be the obvious solution. The last four families to live there were as follows. Mrs Sanderson, a pleasant, rosy-faced widow – who was always referred to as the landlady. She always kept a few hens, but took the precaution of raising her poultry house on stilts. The Redden family resided there for many years and, when the place was flooded, Mr Redden would wade out using two chairs as stilts – no wellies in those days. There was also the Hunter family; but the last to leave were Mr Albert Grey, his wife and young family. I can remember them moving into Oliver Crescent in 1938, three years after this small new Council Estate was completed. The old skinnery was then left to tumble down. Steel spikes can still be seen in the tall old willow trees that stood near these houses – presumably used to attach the washing lines.

Just one field east of the skinnery were the four Paradise Farm Cottages – converted into two about fifty years ago. I can remember them housing the Hill House farm workers in the late 'twenties. Mr Charlie Johnson was head man and Billy Napper was milk lad, delivering milk around Ludworth and Thornley for the Raines. The Charnock family occupied one of the cottages at one stage; I went to school with Ivy, but her brother Fred was somewhat older than myself. These cottages, along with a few acres, were recently sold off, no longer needed for a declining agriculture. Poor old Paradise and its surrounding few acres were recently described as 'a deserted hell hole hiding behind an overgrown hedge' – but there has been an improvement to one house recently.

The remains of Low Croft House Farm can still be seen adjoining the footpath which leads across the fields from the east end of Shadforth to the top of Paradise Bank. It was a small farmstead, last occupied about 1900 by a farmer called Vickers who was one of the well-known farmers and auctioneers of Tow Law.

Mr George Henry Gilson, formerly of High Croft House Farm and now in his ninety-third year, can remember when milk was produced at this small farm and delivered around Ludworth by means of a donkey carrying two milk churns, one strapped either side, from which the milk was measured into people's jugs or cans. The buildings and gin mill can just be recognised from the six pillars which once supported the circular roof, proof that this was a gin-gan, or gin wheel. This was an ancient method of using real horse-power when walking in a circle to turn a huge horizontal wooden wheel (the gin wheel), thereby turning a steel shaft which in turn drove a stationary threshing machine in the adjoining barn, before the advent of the combustion engine.

When the Vickers family left, about 1900, the land became part of the adjoining Ox Close Farm. According to my father, some people called Langley then lived in the house. They did seasonal farm work in the area. Mrs Langley and her daughter also sold flowers and vegetables around Shadforth from a barrow. These were grown in their own garden, which can still be seen to this day, abandoned and surrounded by an overgrown hedge by the side of the footpath. According to the Burial Records, Mrs Langley of Low Croft House died in 1914, aged eighty years. The house was then occupied, for a short time, by someone named Wild, and then it was eventually abandoned about 1930. The old farm ruin is still often referred to as 'Langleys'.

Within a stone's throw of Running Waters Quarry entrance from the A181, at the garage, there were in my time two viable small tenanted farms, both of about eighty acres. The Gilsons reared a family of ten on their farm. Gordon's father, Willie Gilson, of 'Longmyers', of threshing day's fame, being one of seven sons. This farm, 'Running Waters West Farm', was situated on the west side of the quarry entrance. Another brother eventually occupied the Three Horse Shoes. According to my father, this small farm boasted a gin-gan in its day – and a very temperamental milk pony aptly, named Scamp: he was used by the Gilsons to retail milk around Sherburn Hill seventy years ago, but apparently this was only possible when he was on a 'good day'! All too often, he had a bad day, whereupon he would kick the front out of any milk float just for fun! On a good day, he was reputed to be the fastest milk pony in the East. There is little trace of this farmstead today.

My grandparents, the Foords, farmed the Running Waters East Farm, on the opposite side of the quarry entrance, at the same time. Foords also had a large family, nine children, my father being the youngest – thank goodness for today's family planning. My grandfather and family worked the lime quarry as well as the farm. All the stone was hand-filled in those days, then brought to the kilns in horse drawn carts. It was burnt by putting, alternately, a one-foot layer of coke then a three-foot layer of stone all the way up the kiln.

Mr Lon Farley of Cold Knuckles Farm with horse and cart
[Betty Dodd]

The fire was never allowed to go out and the burnt lime was drawn out at the bottom of the kiln by shovel. Two cartloads made a ton and it was normally delivered by two carts, the horse drawing the second cart being hitched to the leading cart by a neck-strap, thereby needing only one driver. My father said that, as the two farms were very close together, the families often joined forces on long winter nights to work on 'clippy mats' on their frames and to make their own entertainment in each other's houses. The families being of similar ages, this worked well and demonstrated a neighbourliness which is rare today. According to my father, this small farm was owned by Mr John Gibson's grandfather of Sherburn Farm and was won on a single bet at a race meeting. Of course, it would be hundreds, rather than thousands, of pounds – we're talking about eighty years ago. My grandparents eventually retired and came to live in Shadforth in 1915. My father was offered the tenancy of Dene House Farm by the Church Commissioners, in the same year.

Cold Knuckles Farm, about eighty acres, has been farmed by the Gilchrist family for longer than I can remember. Edwin's grandfather made a living from it, as many small farmers did in those days. Sadly, in common with all the other previously mentioned small farms in the parish, only a mound of rubble and an overgrown stackyard hedge mark the spot where once stood a viable farm. The land is now farmed by Edwin Gilchrist from Crime Rigg. Mr Lon Farley and his wife Bella were the last of the great country-loving people to live on Cold Knuckles and tend those inland acres for the Gilchrists, just two more victims of the 'agricultural revolution'.

Three fields west of Shadforth and about three hundred yards northeast of Cold Knuckles Farm, the foundation of the old corn mill are just about discernible. Up to about the 1900s, it was driven by a water wheel. The mill and a single-storey house were all one building, and it was owned by the land and coal owner Thomas Crawford, who lived at Littletown House, where he died in 1887, leaving seven daughters and two sons. One son, Thomas, went to America as a young man; the other son, Robert, lived at the mill with his family until he died in 1916. Robert's widow and family finally left the mill in 1925. It was then left to tumble down. Mallander Crawford, Robert's son, was the last to be born at the mill and now lives at Churchill Terrace. A grandson, Ivan Smith, lives at Shadforth.

For a long time, people wondered how the wheel was driven, as the beck passes the site at a lower level than the mill. However, it seems that the water was collected, during wet weather, about three hundred yards upstream in a sort of reservoir area, near some tall willow trees, and was channelled into a sluice where it was stored – to be used as required. The mill race is still just discernible behind the mill site – as a slight gully running approximately south towards an area which is now marshy. A reserve water supply came from what was locally known as 'Gilson's Pond', quite a distance away to the southwest. It was conveyed via an open ditch – but that was a long time ago.

For they were surely the golden years . . . Stan Foord remembers

***SLS News* 8** April 1994

In Shadforth alone I have witnessed the loss of eleven trades people and, in Shadforth Parish, no less than ten small farmsteads. As well as two mines, Sherburn Hill Co-op, the school, the post office, the Methodist chapel and two small sweet shops. They once provided work for all three villages and all within walking distance of their place of work. In direct contrast with today, when the whole workforce of our village leave each morning, mostly one to a car, for their place of work miles away.

As with most small villages over the past fifty years, Shadforth has lost most of its rural charm. Only St Cuthbert's Church and the Plough Inn remain.

Farmsteads in Shadforth Parish (all gone in my lifetime)

Fat Close Farm	*Ralph Blench, G W Eley*
Cold Knuckles Farm	*W Gilchrist*
Strawberry Hill Farm	*W Dobson, F W Long*
High Croft House Farm	*Harry Oliver, G H Gilson*
Running Waters West Farm	*J A Gilson*
Running Waters East Farm	*John Foord, G Flower*
West Farm	*G Flower, F W Long*
Low Croft House Farm	*T H Vickers*
Bourne House Farm	*T M Oliver, S Shepherd*
Dene House Farm	*H J Patterson, S W Foord*

Trades people in Shadforth village (all gone in my lifetime)

builder (stone masons)	*Whittingham Bros*
lamp oil (retail)	*S A Joice*
blacksmith	*T M Oliver*
cartwright and joiner	*Brown Bros*
undertaker	*R F Thubron (Senior)*
cartwright and joiner	*R F Thubron (Junior)*
Saddle Inn	*Ivan McRoy R F Thubron (Junior)*
pig killer	*Tom Hutchinson*
post office	*Geoff Young, S A Joice*
grocer	*John Morton*
grocer	*S A Joice*

Farming used to be a very satisfying way of life, fifty years ago; one person in four in this country was engaged in agriculture, if we include the associated trades. Now it's only one in seventy.

In the 'thirties, agriculture was our biggest industry, mining was next. It was an old and well worn saying that when the miners prospered farming did likewise, and when they both prospered so did this country.

Just a few of us are old enough to remember the pride and pleasure of ploughing with horses. The feel of the bright steel cutting a straight shiny furrow was so satisfying and close to nature, drawn by a team of well turned-out horses. Then bringing them home from a good day's winter ploughing to a warm stable, bedded knee-deep in clean, white straw, lit by a Hurricane oil lamp while being groomed and fed their final well earned feed. I still have vivid memories of those wonderful horse days, playing cards on the stable corn bin on winter nights to the sound of contented horses munching their hay, or playing quoits in the stackyard with old horse shoes. No television distractions, then.

The friendly endearing attraction of those small stockfarms had a fascination for village lads fifty years ago, there was so much physical work going on that boys wanted to help and often did. But nothing stays the same; by the mid 'forties, those lovely rural scenes began to disappear. Tractors

Stan on the village green in 1982/3, with two year old 'Denehouse Lonely 38th', one of his prize Friesian heifers
[Stan Foord]

were here to stay and, as the horses disappeared, farming began to lose its character.

But, oh! How we miss the craftsmanship of yesteryear, farming and all the associated industries. The jolly horse ploughmen, the stackers, thatchers, hedgelayers, drainers, cartwrights, wheelwrights, saddlers and blacksmiths. The salt of the earth, dedicated countrymen who took a pride in a job well done. I'm not suggesting that we go back to the horses. Time has overtaken them on the large mechanised farms of today.

Hanging above our fireplace, at Dene House, we have a picture of three beautiful heavy Clydesdales horses, standing at the watering trough in the farmyard, just to remind me, not of easier times or more financially rewarding times, but of better more stable and more sensible times. Times when doors and windows could be left unlocked. They were times when people had respect for each other and each other's property, the police, the school teacher and the clergy. *For they were surely the golden years.*

Footnote Having worked with farm animals all my life, and being a pedigree breeder of British Friesian Dairy cattle most of it, I still marvel at their good behaviour compared with some human beings! In the twilight of my life, my most treasured moments are spent observing the wonderful wild life out in the open country, away from the self-made human tragedies. *Stan Foord 2006*

Stan Foord, in 'Dene House', with grandson Jack. The painting of the Clydesdale horses hangs above the fireplace
[Stan Foord]

SLS News Editor's note *A word of thanks to Stan Foord, not only for his interesting articles on life in Shadforth over the years, but also for the terrific job he has done, 'tidying up' through the village. It's a long time since the 'edges and verges' of Shadforth looked so tidy. Other people have done similar work to a lesser degree in the past and Stan has shown how much he cares for Shadforth in a very practical way. Thanks Stan.*

Post office, shops, trades and public houses

Post office

Shadforth, being a small village, did not have a wide variety of shops, but one of the main outlets was the post office. The first reference to a post office in Shadforth is in 1849 (Post Office Archives). It closed in 1865 and re-opened in 1893, finally closing again in 1978. Mr John Thursby was the postmaster in the 1860s, Mr Jeffrey Young in the 1920s and Mrs E I Joice in the 1930s, according to sources from the history book by William Whellan and Kelly's Directories.

The post office apparently occupied a number of sites in the village. One lady can remember living in what had been the post office at Top End in 6 Brown's Buildings. The final site of the post office was at 19 North Side, on the sharp corner in the centre of the village. The post office was undoubtedly a popular shop, selling virtually everything, and was a central venue for a chat, as residents recall:

All the village gossip took place there, while the villagers sat on empty pop bottle crates.

The post office sold everything – bread, sweets in old-fashioned jars, tins of peas, carrots, whatever, and washing powder. In the post office, I can remember an old round stamp and thick black pad that you used for stamping postal orders. The post office section had a glass partition, but it wasn't separate from the rest of the shop as it would be now. There was only ever Cissie serving in the shop.

This photograph shows what we believe to be the house before it was converted into the post office, as shown in the photograph overleaf. A large stone, possibly the mounting stone, can be seen in both pictures
[Bill Errington]

Shadforth post office in the 1930s. It is now a private house
[Brenda Jameson]

One young girl remembers her mother, who ran the pub:

... dashing across the road for a loaf of bread and keeping a watch on the door of the pub at the same time, in case anyone went in.

Bread from the post office was delivered to residents in Shadforth by a young schoolgirl, who remembers it vividly:

I had a bogey pram chassie, maroon in colour, with sides built up and concave roof, a pram handle at one side and, at the other side, little double doors that opened and inside two real wooden bread trays that slid out. Cissie would write out the names of who the bread was to go to. She wrote on the back of bits of cardboard or sweet boxes. Whichever route you were doing, whether it was the Council houses or the village, you used to put the bread in, according to the list. Then, once you had got it loaded, you set off. You knocked on all the doors and handed in the bread. There were very few people who said to leave it on the step. Sometimes, you would leave it with a next-door neighbour, if they were in, because I delivered after school or Saturday mornings. I pushed this barrow around, then back to the shop for the next load, and that was four nights a week and Saturday mornings for a quarter of sweets and eleven shillings a week. You could have any sweets in the shop ... but she used to point you to the not so dear ones! You didn't step out of line with her!

The post office would take orders on a Monday and deliver to the house on a Thursday.

Sam Joice used to deliver paraffin. The paraffin was stored in a big separate building, to the side of the post office. He had a four-wheel horse-drawn trailer, with a tank of paraffin, to sell to residents of Shadforth, Ludworth and Thornley.

The last postmistress was Mrs J Taylor, who gave up the business in 1978. The post office is now a private house, but still has the post-box in the wall.

Shops and trades

William Whellan's book on the history of Durham and Kelly's Directories give a good indication of the type of skills residents of Shadforth had in the 19th century. The list below is an example of the tradesmen and women in the village.

Rev R G L Blenkinsopp	parson
John Brown	joiner and blacksmith
John Carter	butcher
Richard Earle	fellmonger
Edward Fraimes	painter and glazier
Robert Harrison	boot and shoemaker
Michael Hills	shopkeeper
Thomas Humes	beer retailer
Thomas Johnson	butcher
Thomas Moore	farm bailiff
John Nicholson	blacksmith
Ann Pattison	shopkeeper
Joseph Robinson	tailor
John Thursby	tailor, postmaster
James Walker	butcher
William Wallace	boot and shoemaker
Robert Whittingham	stone-mason

There were other small outlets in the village over the years. There was a sweet shop near the 'Corner Cupboard' on South Side, along the lane to the Dene. It was run by two sisters, Mary and Bella Ferguson. One resident remembers a little story:

A boy went to Bella, having been told by his mother to ask if they had anything in the eating line. He said, 'Have you owt on the line to eat?'

There was another little sweet shop that people remember, next to the Plough.

The site where the village hall is now was originally a chapel, then a reading room and then a shop owned by Mr Tom Morton, who sold groceries. One resident remembers it being part derelict and colonised by pigeons. Mr Morton also had a horse and flat cart, taking groceries to homes and farms.

John Morton, his wife and one of his sons, Jack. John had a small shop near the Plough
[Mabel Smith]

Mr Charnock recalls working for Tommy Morton, in his *Shadforth, Ludworth and Sherburn Hill Community News* article:

His [Tommy's father, John] little shop, which was only a house window, was about two doors from the Plough Inn. It was run for him by his daughter, Mrs Janet Brown, and his son, Tommy. Tommy later acquired larger premises. He used to deliver to the outlying farms, etcetera. He would start a boy just leaving school. A horse would be borrowed from Peter Raine and the deliveries made. One such boy was Ernie Kendal. Tommy paid him two shillings and sixpence a week (approximately thirteen pence in today's money). Six months later, my friend, Bill Napper, left school. Tommy collared him for two shillings (or ten pence). Later, Billy started working for Peter Raine and Tommy got me for one shilling and a packet of sweets, which he carefully weighed.

One Saturday evening, I tried to make myself look presentable before going to Thornley Hippodrome. I went to Tommy for my shilling. He carefully weighed out my sweets, as usual, and, as he slid them along the counter, he said, 'There thou is. Thou hasn't done very much this week. I'll just give thou a packet of sweets …'

Some residents remember Mrs Crow at the Saddle, which had been a former public house, selling Fox's biscuits from her front room. She was also remembered for her lovely baking.

The Thubron family were, at various times, cartwright, joiner and undertaker. One man remembers:

On the west side of the Saddle Inn was a shop where coffins were made. Mr Thubron was the undertaker. He had three daughters. They used to hide in the coffins during Hide and Seek.

In the 1960s, there was an ice cream factory in what is now known as 'The Cottage'. This building was originally a workshop for the Whittingham Brothers, who were builders and stone masons. The ice cream business was started by Mr Edwin Thirlwell, who became known as 'Mr Whippy'. Yoghurt production can also be remembered by some residents.

The Whittingham family were local builders and stone-masons, employing up to twelve men at one time and responsible for building and maintaining most of the buildings in Shadforth. Many residents rented their homes from the Whittinghams. The family sold up in the 1970s and moved away.

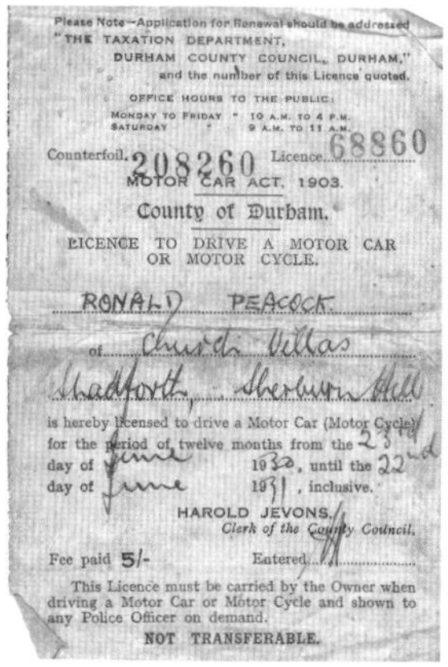
Please Note—Application for Renewal should be addressed
"THE TAXATION DEPARTMENT,
DURHAM COUNTY COUNCIL, DURHAM,"
and the number of this Licence quoted.
OFFICE HOURS TO THE PUBLIC:
MONDAY TO FRIDAY " 10 A.M. TO 4 P.M.
SATURDAY " 9 A.M. TO 11 A.M.
Counterfoil. 208260 Licence. 68860
MOTOR CAR ACT, 1903.
County of Durham.
LICENCE TO DRIVE A MOTOR CAR OR MOTOR CYCLE.
RONALD PEACOCK
of Church Villas
Shadforth, Sherburn Hill
is hereby licensed to drive a Motor Car (Motor Cycle) for the period of twelve months from the 23rd day of June 1930, until the 22nd day of June 1931, inclusive.
HAROLD JEVONS,
Clerk of the County Council.
Fee paid 5/- Entered
This Licence must be carried by the Owner when driving a Motor Car or Motor Cycle and shown to any Police Officer on demand.
NOT TRANSFERABLE.

'The Cottage' in 1975. Originally a workshop for Whittingham Brothers, it became an ice cream factory in the 1960s
[Des Elston]

Ronnie Peacock was a driver for Whittingham Brothers of Shadforth around 1940, their name proudly displayed on the side of the lorry. above **Ronnie's driving licence**
[Brenda Jameson]

left **Workmen of Shadforth, employed by the local builders, Whittingham Brothers, in around 1927/8**
back row, left to right
Bill Errington, Harold Bradley, Ezra Smith, Benny Bradley
front row, left to right
Albert Blanch, Jim York, Ronnie Peacock
[Monica Armstrong / Bill Wood / Brenda Jameson]

There was a blacksmith's shop at Bourne House. Mr Peacock was the blacksmith, and children remembered:

. . . watching him shoe the horses with sizzling all around the legs.

The Co-operative Store was based at Sherburn Hill, and it would deliver to people in Shadforth. A lady describes how it worked:

Sherburn Hill Co-operative Wholesale Society was a godsend – the store'. Nearly everyone joined. Everything, from food to furniture, could be bought or ordered from here. Each family had their own store dividend number, which was quoted at every purchase. The order man visited homes at the beginning of the week to see what provisions were needed, and these were listed and delivered in boxes from a horse drawn cart on Friday evenings. A store butcher came with meats on a cart twice a week. Draperies and footwear could be taken home from the store on 'appro' (approval) for two or three days. A furniture club account could be taken out and a fixed weekly amount paid off. Every quarter, a dividend, according to profits, was paid to members on their purchases. For many who could pay their way comfortably, this dividend became their life savings but, to others, it was a cash bonus to be queued for on dividend day and spent!

Greengrocer Sid Shepherd in 1963. Christine Chapman is at the wheel, with John Shepherd sitting beside her; Jimmy Slater stands by the door

[Monica Armstrong]

There were also lots of independent travelling shopkeepers. Kenny Williamson had a travelling shop, based opposite the post office on North Side. Sid Shepherd had a horse-drawn vehicle, from which he sold fruit and vegetables. He had the garage next to the post office.

He used to come round the village on Tuesdays and Saturdays. Mam used to get all her fruit and veg from him. There was 'young Sid', as he was called, and a lad called Jimmy Slater used to help him out – they came round for years. You used to come out with your bucket – to put potatoes in – or a bag to put fruit in.

Someone else remembers:

Store carts would come round on Monday; you'd say what you want and the four-wheel cart would come down on Friday. There used to be a hole in the hedge by the Council houses and, once, the store horse went over to the grass and the cart turned over and all the groceries went over the road – scrambled egg all over everything!

The Co-op had a store butcher, a baker and a two-horse cart with groceries that came round once or twice a week. Jack Cole was the travelling Co-op man.

Mr John Carter had a horse and cart with fruit and vegetables in the 1930s. One child at the time remembers:

I remember Mr Carter coming round with vegetables. My treat every week was a bar of McGowan's toffee (a big cow on the paper) and a quarter of peanuts. We would sit on the bank and enjoy them.

A young Billy Gustard drove a horse and cart for Mrs Jamieson's bakery. Billy Edgar and Fred Blanch were the butchers.
Mr Whittle from Ludworth sold turnips from a horse and cart. One lady remembers:

I used to get the bus to Durham with a bowl to get ice cream from the Vaudeville, an ice cream parlour on North Road. It was almost melted by the time I got home! Then Baldasera's started to come round in a van. They had a shop in Thornley and used to do a round on Sunday. There was also a travelling hardware van for pans and paraffin oil. The people were called Satley. They also charged the accumulator batteries, which were used to power the radio.

Some women remember the early Avon ladies coming around the doors.

There were two Avon ladies, Mrs Crow for the lower end of the village and Mrs Maughan for the top end.

Public houses

At one time, in the 1860s, there were five public houses in Shadforth: the Plough, the Saddle Inn, the Wheatsheaf, the Red Lion and the Black Horse. The Plough is the only pub that remains in Shadforth today. Some people can still remember the Saddle Inn, and there is an old photograph of the building as a working pub. It is now a private house called The Old Saddle.

One of the main memories people have of the Plough is of the South Durham Hunt, which assembled outside the building. On one old photograph from 1908, the hunt is shown outside Dene House Farm, but most residents agree that this would not have happened in their lifetime, and possibly the photograph was set up. Certainly, photographs from the 1960s show the horses outside the Plough. There is a stone outside the Plough, which was used in the past to help riders mount and dismount from their horses.

Most people's memories of the Plough are during the 1960s, when Jack and Janet Watson ran the pub. Their daughter, Gwen, was born just before the outbreak of the Second World War, and she recalls her mother's memory:

The Saddle Inn in around 1910. It is now a private house
[Bill Errington]

The Plough Inn in the 1950s. The only pub now left in the village
[Gwen Robson]

above and right **In the late 1960s, the South Durham Hunt would always gather outside the Plough Inn**
[Gwen Robson]

above **The bar of the Plough Inn in the late 1940s or early 1950s** left to right (**unidentified**), **Fred Ingleby, Joe Watson, Sid Shepherd, Tommy Kendle** partly hidden**, Billy Ollet, George Williamson, Wilf Scullion, Jack Watson,** (**unidentified**) [Gwen Robson]

Mum was in bed, having me, and grandfather, who I never knew, was standing with his back to us, looking out the window, with his hands behind his back, swinging on his feet, saying, 'Well, Janet, you've got a new baby girl and war has just been declared.'

The left hand side of the Plough, where the public bar is now, was a stable at one time. Gwen remembers her dad keeping his motorbike in there. There were cobbles outside the stable so that the horses did not slip. There was a mounting-stone outside to help people onto their horses, and hooks on the wall to fasten the reins.

The main door at that time was in the middle of the pub, where it went straight through to the back, like a corridor. The front door would be hooked open and the middle door inside had a sneck, so you could tell if someone walked in. There was a black stove set on a square of tiles on the floor. Gwen remembers soldiers coming to the pub:

One soldier propped his gun or rifle against the corner of the bar and it toppled over and smashed the tiles. Mum wasn't pleased!

When the Watsons took on the pub, there was lino on the floor in the bar and a sawdust trough around the counter. Sometimes, drinkers would throw away their cigarette ends in the sawdust, which would catch fire, and Mr Watson would have to throw a glass of water across it.

There were lots of pictures and stuffed animals in the pub that had been done by Bob Lofthouse, the famous naturalist and taxidermist from Ludworth.

The newly refurbished bar inside the Plough Inn in 1964
left to right **Janet Watson, Barrie Robson, Gwen Robson, Jack Watson**
[Gwen Robson]

Gwen recalls women sitting in what was her mother's kitchen or living room.

It was a licensed room – it had a number '3' on the door. There was a sink, a cooking range, a pantry, sofa and chairs, and women would drink in there. I used to get a tray and ask what they wanted to drink. I used to go down to the cellar and my dad would tip a bucket upside down for me to put the tray on. For four pints, I would half fill the pint glasses, then turn the tap off. When it came to topping-off, you had to lift the tray so the nozzle of the tap actually went inside the glass, otherwise the froth would come over the top of the glass, and my dad would do that bit. Sally would play the piano and everyone would sing.

Another child at the time remembers:

The left side was always the beer bar and the lounge was on the right. Women never ever went in the bar, always the lounge. Further through the room, on the right, was a door to Jack Watson's sitting room. We used to go in for crisps and we always had to go in the middle and knock on the bar door until they heard us – we never ever went in!

There was generally a good community spirit in those days. However, some women did not like their husbands drinking and would come knocking on the door to get their husbands back, and one woman even phoned the police.

The pub was tied to a brewery, originally Westoe Breweries of South Shields, then they were taken over by Bass. Gwen's father allowed dominoes and darts in the pub, but never cards – she does not know why. Also, he would never have politics or religion discussed, as it caused arguments.

Children growing up in the 1980s recall village life and the lack of amenities:

One thing difficult to ignore, however, was the lack of amenities in Shadforth. Shadforth's last shop (the post office) closed just before the 1980s, leaving the Plough as the sole retail outlet, but no use for younger members of the village! A green greengrocer's van, ice-cream van and a butcher's van did visit the village every week. We bought 'ninety-nines' with 'monkey's blood' from the ice cream van, and plastic cones of ice-cream with bubble gum in the bottom, but my favourite was the butcher's, as he always gave us sweets ('midget gems', I think), even though he knew we were unlikely customers. We remember the traditional red phone box in front of the post office, which has now sadly been replaced by a newer model. We are still hoping that someone will open a shop – and a new ice-cream factory!

A coach trip from the Plough Inn in the 1940s or 1950s
[Mary Cairns]

Shadforth Women's Institute

Shadforth Women's Institute was formed in 1947, thirty-two years after the first WI was formed in Britain. The institute was the brainchild of Mrs H Gibbons, Mrs D Stonehouse and Mrs R Short. Thirty-five members attended the first meeting and Mrs Bage was elected first president – an office she held for eleven years.

When the WI began, the meetings were held in the village school. This was considered an inadequate meeting-place, and the WI lent its weight to the building of the village hall. They played a big part in raising money for materials, by organising 'bring and buy' sales, whist drives and sales of work, and raised over £100 for the roof.

In the late 1940s, before the village hall had been built, Shadforth Women's Institute had to meet in the village school
[Gwen Robson]

When the Women's Institute celebrated its fifteenth birthday, it was described as having a 'strong family atmosphere. Everybody in the village knows everyone else.'
Durham County Advertiser 2nd March 1962
[Ethel Stout]

An article appeared in the *Durham County Advertiser* on 2nd March 1962, which reported on the celebrations of the fifteenth birthday party of the Shadforth Women's Institute:

'Shadforth is a very small village, with only 140 houses, yet out of this small community has come a most vital women's institute, whose only impediment to spectacular progress is an understandable lack of younger members. The

Shadforth WI in 1973
Durham County Advertiser
[Ethel Stout]

pleasure all the ladies derive from their institution is infectious and the family atmosphere of Shadforth WI is something that larger institutes have every right to envy.'

The slight worry expressed in this article about the lack of younger members has probably proved true, to some extent. Shadforth Women's Institute still exists, although membership is now only at nineteen, but its members remain very active with a full programme of events.

Shadforth WI in 1996, still dressing up and having fun
[Ian Thompson]

A tea party in Shadforth, possibly in 1935 to celebrate the Royal Silver Jubilee of King George V and Queen Mary, or in 1937 for the coronation of King George VI

Epilogue

William Whellan wrote, in 1894:

The village of Shadforth is situated in a valley, through which the Shadforth Beck flows westward to the Wear, about five miles east-south-east from Durham. As it is enclosed by steep hills, much of its old rural character has been preserved, and it forms a striking contrast to the pit villages in the neighbourhood.

Ursula Patrickson wrote, in the early 1940s:

The village of Shadforth, which comes into my area, has a small population composed chiefly of agricultural workers, although miners live there who work at Sherburn Hill Colliery. It is essentially an agricultural village unspoilt by the influence of industry. As one enters the village, one is reminded of what the small villages must have been like in former days. The houses are clustered around the village green, many buildings are very old, such as the Church School and the old inns. An old world air is lent to the village by a water-wheel and a windmill, which still remains at the bottom of the village. Like Sherburn, there are several farms in the village itself and there is a pleasant smell of hay and earth as one passes up the main road on to the hill.

Ian Thompson reflects, in 2006:

The character of our village has changed somewhat over the years. Shadforth Beck still flows through the village, but the miners, many agricultural workers and local businesses have gone. Modern machines now harvest the fields and dust is still blown in the wind, reminiscent of years gone by. In fact, although Shadforth has become a dormitory village, when there is a lull in the traffic you can almost imagine life in any era. Although we are now in the twenty-first century, there is a timeless quality to the village of Shadforth.

Sources

Roberts, Brian K, 1977
The Green Villages of County Durham
Durham County Library Local History Publication no 12

Durham County Record Office
Shadforth School Governors' and Managers' Minutes E/C/C11

Durham County Record Office
Shadforth School Log Books E/C 50–3

Edwards, Elaine
A History of Shadforth C E School

Gilchrist Family Diaries

Granlund, C G, 1987
Socio-economic change in County Durham, 1880 to the present. Rural change in a Durham village

Kelly's Directories

Ursula Patrickson, early 1940s
A geographical survey of the area embracing: Sherburn Hill, Sherburn, Sherburn House and Shadforth in the County of Durham

Shadforth, Ludworth and Sherburn Hill Community News

Shadforth Parish Magazine

Wheatley Hill History Club
The Thornley Coal Company owners of Thornley, Ludworth and Wheatley Hill collieries 1830–1885

William Whellan and Co, 1856 and 1894
History of the County Palatine of Durham

Conclusion

Shadforth History Group was formed in July 2004. Helen Grindley was the initiator of the group. She provided the incentive and impetus to carry out the tasks needed to produce the end result – this book.

Much willing help was given by the rest of the group: Judy McLean, Anne Rowe, Donald and Moira Tate, Ian Thompson, Stuart Watt and Bill Wood. Many thanks for their endeavours.

Much of the members' time has been taken up by historical research, interviews with local people and group studies attended. The bulk of effort behind the scenes – clerical work and negotiation to finance the project, as well as printing and, not least, the exhibitions held – fell mainly upon Helen's shoulders.

Perhaps the most interesting parts of the book lie in those sections which include quotes from interviews with the older inhabitants of the village. The genuine warmth of Shadforth people, in days gone by, is very apparent in their personal accounts. It comes through their memories like the glow from an open fire in an old country cottage.

Their hard lives, with little money, presented many problems. These were somewhat eased by their great community spirit, which stemmed from having to deal with such difficult times, and that is a great tribute to them. We are grateful for their co-operation.

We would like to thank everyone who has agreed to talk to us and share their past with us.

Bill Wood 2006

Acknowledgements

We are grateful to the following people for their contribution to the history project and help in producing this book.

Elaine Avery
Monica Armstrong
Alan Atkinson
Clare Blake
Fred and Doreen Blanch
Albert Blanch
Harry and Betty Brass
John and Mary Cairns
Fred Charnock
Avis Clarke
William Dobson
Betty Dodd
Edith Drummond
Durham County Record Office
Des Elston
Bill Errington
Stan and Evelyn Foord
Edwin Gilchrist
Chris Giles
Gordon and Kathleen Gilson
Vera Goodwin
Les and Alice Granlund
Colin Granlund
Helen Grindley
Julie Hawthorn
Harold Henderson
Simon Hunt
Margaret Iveson
Brenda Jameson
Tom Johnson
Frank and Ivy Johnston
Olive Langan
Bill and Susan Laycock
Mary Lowes
Louise McEnaeny
Judy McLean
George Nairn
Margaret Nancarrow
Jean and Colin Ord
Sylvia Pritchard
Peggy Redden
Barrie and Gwen Robson
Betty Robinson
Ellis and Anne Rowe
Noel Sharpe
Betty Smith
David Smith
Frank and Jane Smith
Gordon and Mabel Smith
Dorothy Stead
Ethel Stout
Nora Strong
Joyce St Julien
Mary Sturdy
Donald and Moira Tate
Heather Thompson
Ian and Beryl Thompson
John Thompson
Lara Thompson
Peter Thompson
Christina Unwin
Mr Walton
Pat Warren
Stuart and Marjorie Watt
Sheila and Tony Wilson
Bill and Edna Wood
Phyl Yard